KU-013-129

contemporary lighting

SEBASTIAN CONRAN & MARK BOND

special photography by Thomas Stewart

644.3   i0064085

Luton Sixth Form College
Learning Resources Centre

To Sam, Max & Lola – light of our lives

WITHDRAWN

Luton Sixth Form College
Learning Resources Centre

Pandora Books
644.3
£5.99

contemporary lighting

WITHDRAWN

10064085

Luton Sixth Form College

contents

And God said, Let there be light: # and there was light.

And God saw the light, that it was good: and God divided the light from the darkness.

And God called the light Day, and the darkness he called Night. And the evening and the morning were the first day.

introduction

There is more to light than meets the eye.

'God is light, and in him is no darkness at all' (John 1). The Bible is crammed with similar divine-like positive references to light, as well as negative ones to darkness. There are also indications in many other ancient texts that our forebears had a strong attitude and spiritual relationship to light. These days, we know that through photosynthesis it is light that in fact gives life ... well, if it does not exactly give life, it definitely allows life to continue. From a more secular scientific perspective, light is earth's principal source of natural, renewable energy from which all life stems. Without it, plant life and therefore animal life could not survive for long.

Light travels at 300 million metres per second, the fastest attainable speed yet known to man. It is also the scientific absolute that relates to time. Whether you are interpreting Albert Einstein's theories of relativity or Stephen Hawking's 'light cones' there does not appear to be anything beyond light. In fact, as far as I can fathom from their complex arguments, if you were to go faster than light you would theoretically be going back in time – or whatever else hyper-space promises – light years from now.

Light also communicates our surroundings to us – this is the familiar visible light that bounces off objects into our eyes. Natural daylight from the sun consists of a cocktail of different coloured wavelengths that blend

Our design studio was originally designed to give maximum natural light for working. Now we have to use computers the ambient light needs subduing – a sad reflection on technology.

The Shadow Collection, designed by Marcel Wanders in 1998 for Cappellini. The exaggerated scale of this floor light is clearly a comment on the traditional table light. This light, however, is composed from a translucent composite film hung over a skeletal metal rod frame with incandescent bulbs both in the shade and the stem. The effect is an even, glowing, ambient light, which works particularly well against a wall or to open up a corner.

There is clear scientific evidence that light profoundly affects the psychology, spirit, emotions and mood. This is most pronounced in territories near the poles such as Scandinavia and Iceland, where there is very little natural daylight for much of the winter. Consequently, in these countries there is a high incidence of cyclic clinical depression.

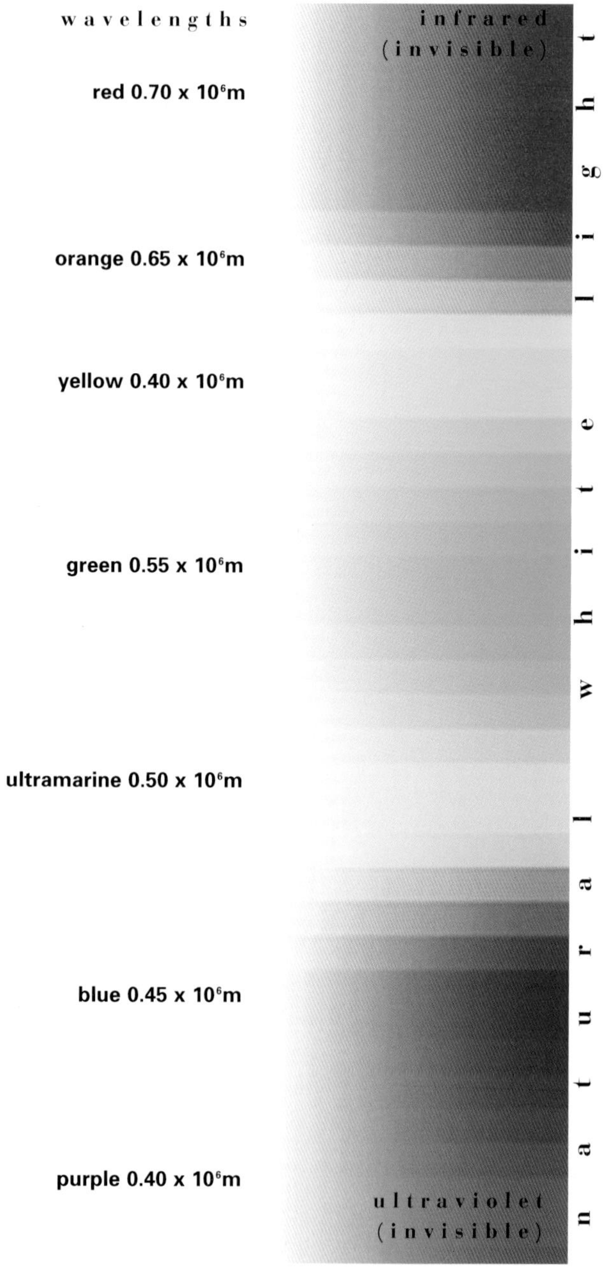

wavelengths

infrared (invisible)

red 0.70 x 10^{6}m

orange 0.65 x 10^{6}m

yellow 0.40 x 10^{6}m

green 0.55 x 10^{6}m

ultramarine 0.50 x 10^{6}m

blue 0.45 x 10^{6}m

purple 0.40 x 10^{6}m

ultraviolet (invisible)

light

white

natural

together in what we perceive as 'white' light. We may take it for granted, but imagine life without it, without sight – most of what we know comes through our eyes.

Scientifically speaking, light is generally a product of intense heat exciting molecules of matter to such an extent that they rid themselves of energy by radiating it as light. The different chemical elements tend to give off individual wavelengths (their spectrographic signature) but generally, the hotter the source, the 'brighter' the light. Therefore all lamps give off different quantities and qualities of light with subtly different properties depending on what they are made from and how they are constructed and powered. Accordingly, they are each suitable for different applications. The reason for this is that none can give as broad a spectrum of light as the light derived from the extremes of the on-going nuclear fission of the sun.

As a general rule, the higher the temperature of a light-source, the more spectrographic bias to the shorter (bluer) wavelengths of the light. In other words, proportionally less infrared gives a broader light which brings out the blues as well as the reds intrinsic to any object bathed in it. It does get a little more complex, as the ingredients of the spectrographic cocktail of each type of light are not equally proportional, but this is not the place to go into it.

Here is a pertinent example: candlelight has a higher proportion of warm coloured long wavelength than moonlight, which has a bias to cooler looking shorter wavelengths. Hence warm rich reds and skin tones look better in candlelight than in bright moonlight, despite the intensities being similar. Likewise, sunlight has a very broad colour spectrum whereas a fluorescent tube is narrow (this is where it makes its energy saving). An example of narrow waveband light is the yellow low-pressure sodium lights used on motorways. These are particularly efficient in terms of output brightness but across a very narrow spectrographic band. Colour temperatures of various sources are typically:

Until the Second World War, acetylene gas was used in portable lamps on early bicycles and motorcars. This was because it provided a relatively high intensity light because acetylene burns at a much higher temperature than town gas. Acetylene gas can also be created by dripping water on easily portable calcium carbide granules, as shown here where Tom Dixon is enjoying welding with acetylene gas.

Tungsten filament: 2,500°C
Quartz-halogen: 2,850°C
Fluorescent discharge: 2,900°C
Evening sun: 4,000°C
Cloudy midday: 6,000°C
Bright midday sun: 10,000°C

Objects are coloured according to the wavelengths they absorb and reflect. A brilliant white object, for example, absorbs only about 8 per cent of visible light, reflecting 92 per cent of light shone on it. A matt black object, on the other hand, absorbs about 95 per cent of visible light, reflecting very little. A red apple absorbs green light and reflects red, while a green apple absorbs red and reflects green.

The spectrographic mix of light clearly effects the perception of colours viewed in it. The eye reacts to different colour temperatures too; the colder the light, the smaller the pupil. For example, fluorescent colours appear to glow brighter than their surroundings because they change the wavelength of the short wavelength ultraviolet light that is invisible to the eye when reflecting it, making it longer and therefore more apparent.

getting started

history

There are two predominant forms of light, artificial light from electricity and natural light from the sun. They are about as similar as lead and gold – one makes a poor imitation of the other.

Without some sort of artificial light when darkness fell, early Homo sapiens would have no option but to stop whatever they were doing and sleep. The night in winter would be long and cold, in summer short. The harnessing of light was principally what allowed ancient man to unshackle himself from the routine imposed by nature; maybe the first real step in differentiating ourselves from the beasts.

Until the twentieth century, after dark the world was largely lit by fire. Although electric light had been around as a scientific curiosity since Davy's arc lamp experiments in the early 1800s, it wasn't until 1879 that commercially mass-produced electric light became attainable with the development of the incandescent electric lamp. During that year, Thomas Edison (using screw fittings in the USA) and Joseph Swan (using bayonet fittings in the UK) simultaneously developed a reliable glowing filament, and electric lighting really took off.

The principle of this shared invention was pivotal to the discovery of suitable materials that would conduct electricity producing extreme heat and light when a voltage was applied across them. The filament had to tolerate the white heat required to give good light whilst not disintegrating. After much searching for the right material to use as a filament, legend has it that in Edison's case this was carbonized cotton from a female visitor's garment. This discovery, coupled with the advent of an electricity supply network, redefined the meaning of the word convenience. Now, a 100-watt tungsten filament lamp with over a metre of coiled wire in it can theoretically give the light of 120 candles.

The twentieth century was set to become the century of electric lighting. Initially, the design of these early electric lights was clearly influenced by contemporary lamp and candle stands. Innovative design approaches for the new phenomenon quickly took root, though, as evidenced in the work of the artistic design movements of the era. With the Arts and Crafts, Art Nouveau and the Successionists it soon became apparent that lights could

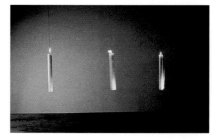

Fly Candle Fly, designed by Georg Baldele. These miniature pendant lights give off an almost ecclesiastical ambience from their small capsule bulbs.

be important decorative objects, early examples of which are the colourful stained glass lampshades emanating from Tiffany Studios in New York. New forms and approaches began to be developed by the other emerging European design styles that made up the Modern Movement such as De Stijl in the Netherlands, Bauhaus in Germany, the Art Deco school and developments in Scandinavia, epitomized by the Danish designer Poul Henningsen (see his evolutionary 1958 *Artichoke* pendant light opposite).

Until recently, domestic lights have entirely depended on incandescent lamps, the constraints of the actual forms available and their need for efficient reflection, direction and also lamp cooling. Some lights have used the lamps as a feature, emphasizing their forms, others try to hide the source from view to reduce glare. The post-war period of the fifties and sixties saw the development of lamps with integrated silvered reflectors which biased the light to make spotlight bulbs. This allowed lights to be made with more compact heads (see *Luminator* on page 31). Taking lamps from other intended sources also became popular, such as low-voltage lamp units from cars (see Castiglioni's *Toio* light on page 45).

Electric light had been around as a scientific curiosity in the early 1800s. However, it wasn't until 1879 that mass-produced electric light became more readily attainable.

In the search to develop a smaller bulb for the automotive industry it was discovered that with the addition of a halogen gas such as bromine or iodine, the tungsten filament's vapour forms a chemical bond with the gas. This is re-deposited back on the filament allowing it to glow at 2,800°C, 250°C past its normal maximum operating temperature. The result is a brighter and 'cooler', more energy-efficient light that is more closely matched to natural light. The quartz glass is also much more resistant to violent temperature fluctuation so the capsule can be made that much smaller to fit in confined spaces.

In the latter part of the twentieth century these quartz-halogen lamps were especially favoured by the retail industry as the inherent lack of heating infrared in the light made them particularly suitable for food applications. The development of the dichroic reflector resulted in jewel-like spot lamps that were attractive to look at, too. These truly beautiful and compact lamps have allowed designers to make even smaller lamp-heads in their lights, which also give a better quality of light. In turn, this has created an even greater freedom in the world of lighting design as we look forward to the new century's developments.

1920
Gerrit Rietvelt

1927
Eileen Grey

1907
Mariano Fortuny Y Madrazo

1932
George Carwardine

1933
Pietro Chiesa

1958
Poul Henningsen

1962
Achille & Pier
Giacomo
Castiglioni

1969
Vico Magistretti

1972
Richard Sapper

bulbs

In its present form, the 'light bulb', as the electrical incandescent filament lamp became known, is something of a design classic, remaining more or less unaltered for almost all the twentieth century. It has become an icon of this era, this is a boast that few industrially produced items can

1 200W mains supply double-ended halogen, *also available as 150-500W.* **2** 150W mains supply halogen *with Edison screw fitting.* **3** 2-pin, 50W halogen capsule *for use with a reflector.* **4** 50W open-fronted dichroic halogen miniature spot *with integrated parabolic reflector available in various beam angles from spot to flood.* **5** 50W miniature mains-voltage halogen spot *that doesn't need a transformer.* **6** Full size flood 30-75W halogen spot *with Edison screw fitting.* **7** 21W compact fluorescent *with integrated ballast and Edison screw fitting.* **8** 2-pin, 16W fluorescent formed tube *available in a variety of sizes.* **9** 4-pin, 22W circular fluorescent tube, *available in a variety of sizes.* **10** 18W compact fluorescent low-energy globe *with integrated ballast with Edison screw fitting.* **11** 7W compact fluorescent single tube, *available in a variety of sizes.* **12** 15W compact fluorescent double tube *with integrated ballast and Edison screw fitting.* **13** 10W pencil thin mini fluorescent single tube, *useful for discreet undershelf lighting.* **14** 15W single tube fluorescent *available in a variety of colour temperatures depending on tonal qualities required. Needs an integrated ballast fitting.* **15** 525mm compacted fluorescent U-tube.

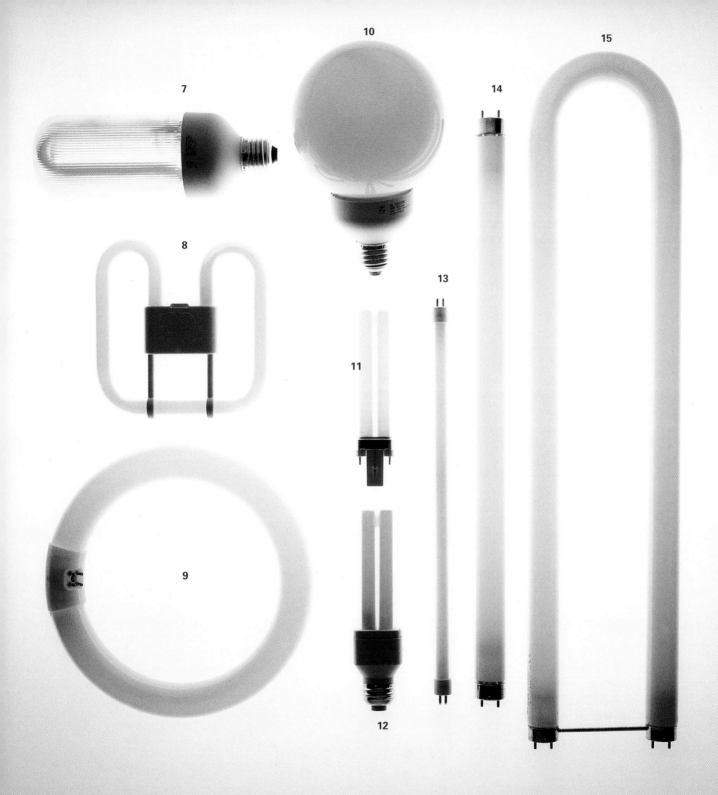

claim. Conventional filament bulbs (expensive tungsten is the best as it lasts longer) have a maximum operating temperature of around 2,500°C before the coiled, metre-long filament starts to vaporize. Also, they have to be quite large otherwise the glass would shatter under the rapid extreme temperature changes caused by switching on and off. But over the last 25 years there have been many interesting technical innovations, such as the introduction of low-voltage quartz-halogen lamps and integrated dichroic reflectors.

Recently, however, the faithful light bulb seems to have fallen from grace. Having once been the coolest hi-tech gizmo of the roaring 1880s (its image even became the universal symbol of a bright idea) the naked bulb subsequently came to represent austerity too. Technology has not stood still, however, and there are now many new alternatives to the familiar vacuous light bulb.

The other ubiquitous light source is the economical-but-bleak fluorescent tube. Once lighting's equivalent of the theoretically practical-but-prosaic low-cost-housing tower-block, due to some sensitive design and technical input it is now rather more acceptable (as is community housing). This lamp produces its light by passing high-voltage electric pulses through a metallic gas (that is usually mercury vapour). This stimulates a discharge of short wavelength (ultraviolet) invisible light that in turn excites the phosphor coating on the tube causing it to fluoresce, radiating visible light.

The positive aspects of the fluorescent tube are that they are extremely energy efficient and can be effectively used to give a good 'even canvas' of ambient light that can be used in conjunction with more focused light sources. There are, however, some less desirable properties. As well as their physical size, they tend to slightly strobe and the colour of the light emitted has a greenish tinge, both of which can be spiritually tiring.

Other principal contenders in the domestic market are, in various forms, the compact fluorescent or the ineptly named 'economy bulb' (who would want to admit to having an economy of style?). Some of the most exciting developments in fluorescent lamps are the pencil thin miniature tubes. The future looks bright too for fibre-optic cables as they can beam a surprisingly bright pool (35W +) of cool light from the tip of a slim cable keeping the bulky power source in a hidden remote location.

When choosing your light bulb, remember that the smaller the point source, the more defined and darker the shadows and the more 'twinkly' the reflections. In addition, the further the source, the sharper the shadow. Conversely, a broad source of light will give more diffuse shadows and softer reflections. Clear glass filament bulbs also give a point source with sharper shadows, whereas opalescent bulbs create more diffuse shadows.

1 100W Blacklite globe bulb *with Edison screw (ES) that has a high ultraviolet output for bringing out those whites.* **2** 60W silver crown ES *that hides the light source, reflecting it back on a parabolic reflector to ensure low spillage from spots.* **3** 40W bayonet fitting opal 'golfball' *incandescent bulb.* **4** 25W mushroom reflector *with small Edsion screw (SES).* **5** 15W pigmy bulb *bayonet fitting.* **6** 40W silver crown with SES. **7** 25W candle flame-shaped bulb with SES. **8** 60W full-size mushroom spot *with bayonet fitting and integrated reflector that suffers slightly from light spillage.* **9** *The classic light bulb – a 60W opal with ES.* **10** 120W spot with ES and *available in different colours. Originally developed for outdoor use, these throw a good beam with little light spillage.* **11** 60W daylight simulation bulb *with bayonet fitting. Gives a better simulation to natural daylight by filtering out much of the warmer spectrum.* **12** 60W integrated reflector spot *with bayonet fitting.* **13** 60W 45mm clear 'golf ball' *with ES.* **14** 25W flicker flame *with small bayonet fitting and oscillating effect to replicate a flickering candle.* **15** 15W ball coloured pigmy bulb *with bayonet fitting.* **16** 25W opal candle bulb *with SES.* **17** 100W high output halogen mushroom reflector *with ES.* **18** 30W, 284mm long clear striplight lamp *used for hidden undershelf lighting.* **19** 60W bayonet fitting *mainly used in candelabra fittings.* **20** 35W twin cap *opal architectural lamp.*

types of lighting

The creative use of light is as much about the use of shadows to give form and drama as about making things blandly visible. This can be supplemented by adding interest using colour, texture and pattern. The practical side of lighting is also concerned with health and safety, particularly in the work place and public areas.

We may think about daylight as a constant, but it varies dramatically depending on the weather, the season, the time of day and the location (the seaside tends to have cleaner, cooler air) – even the latitude has an effect.

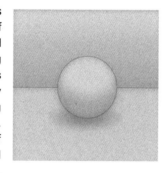

AMBIENT LIGHTING

Ambient light *is similar to the soft, even light that you get on an overcast or cloudy day with very little or no shadow. It is easy to see by but everything looks a little bland without form-defining shadows.*

DOWNLIGHTING

Downlight *is similar in effect to the light received at midday on a cloudless day resulting in intense black shadows. They are usually used in multiples or with some ambient light to colour in the dramatic shadows.*

UPLIGHTING

Uplight *is usually reflected off the walls and the ceiling and is the most flattering form of lighting as it irons out wrinkles and gives the illusion of more space. It can create interesting architectural effects.*

The reason that artists and painters prefer their studios to receive north light is because from the north it has a constant intensity and consistent spectrographic mix. Consequently, the painters' colours then don't change significantly throughout the day.

The degree of artificial lighting required in a room is going to be strongly affected by the intended use of the space coupled with the predominant natural light available. So careful consideration must be given to what the environment to be will look like both at day and at night. Our bodies have been genetically programmed to respond to light levels: an overly bright environment will make us feel alert and wakeful; conversely, subdued light makes us feel more relaxed. Too much bright light for too long makes us feel tense; too much time in subdued light is depressing to the psyche.

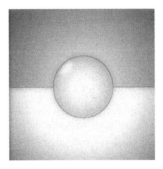

SPOT LIGHTING

Spot lighting *can highlight objects in a dark room, create pools of light on walls or provide useful reading light over seating areas. Spotlights generally need to be used with a reasonably high level of ambient light.*

CANDLE LIGHTING

Candlelight *creates long, hard, flickering shadows, which can be both dramatic and romantic at the same time. The shadows can be softened to good effect if candles are used in multiples around a room.*

TASK LIGHTING

Task lighting *provides a bright pool of light over the task in hand making it easier to see and concentrate. Because of their flexibility, use them to good effect by reflecting the light off walls and surfaces.*

OCCASIONAL LIGHTING

Occasional lights *tend to draw attention to themselves rather than provide useful light, they tend to work best with subdued ambient light when their lighting effect is most noticeable.*

ambient lighting

An over-emphasis of bland surrounding 'ambient' light is not only wasteful but also a little soulless as rooms and objects without defining shadows lack form and character. Conversely, a room full of impenetrable shadows may look dramatic but it is hardly comfortable to live or work in. Instead, some ambient light is pretty much essential for filling out the shadows.

Often ambient lighting is best achieved by reflecting light off the walls (by using ceiling- or floor-mounted wall-washers) or the ceiling (up-lit from the floor or walls). An alternative approach for good ambient lighting is a multiple source such as standard lamps that are casually dotted around the room with large diffusing shades. Go ahead – create light pools where they are needed. Although all rules are to be explored, it is generally a good idea never to make the primary light source (the lamp itself) visible. Instead, always have the bulb diffused or reflected by the shade rather than spilling its glare and attendant harsh shadow.

With the proliferation of computers the requirements for work lighting have recently changed. Rather than needing a pool of bright light on the work surface, subdued, diffused, ambient light minimizing over-spill from primary light sources are preferable to prevent glare or reflections on the display screens.

During the course of a day, a kitchen-dining-room, for example, is used for preparing and eating breakfast, reading the papers, maybe some domestic administration, coffee and a chat, preparing supper, enjoying the evening meal and perhaps indulging in a spot of telly, too. In the morning, the space may be bathed in sunlight from the east and in the evening, have no daylight at all. Flexible lighting is required not just an on/off switch.

Ambient and some task lighting is required for preparing food but then supper will be much more enjoyable – in fact, it will actually taste better – if it is not eaten in the same bright, diffused light. One approach is to have different combinations of lights that you can vary the use of to change the mood. Dimmers are particularly useful for this but check that they are compatible with the light source. You will find that fluorescent lamps and some low-voltage transformers may not perform with dimmers or even cause them permanent damage.

downlighting

The light source for downlighting can be ceiling mounted or ceiling recessed, or can emit from ceiling spots, ceiling edge and corner bulbs, pendants and wall-mounted floods. There is much that lighting can do to change the perceived size and proportions of a space. The most noticeable effect of downlighting is to apparently drop the height of a ceiling. The ceiling is cloaked in shadow and therefore appears to come closer to the viewer.

Always bear in mind the direction of light in relation to the position of the eye. Look at a photograph taken into the sun and then look at the same subject photographed with the sun behind you. The difference could not be more pronounced – in the first the subject is obscured in shadow and in the second it is well lit with all features visible. The position of light is paramount to our perception of the 'subject' that is illuminated. Any half good cricketer, fighter pilot or interrogator will tell you of the advantage of having the light behind your shoulder. Although dramatic and flattering to architecture, light polarized from directly above puts the eyes into shadow giving a hard impression. Having said this, downlights are useful for enlivening dull corridors or hallways. When used in evenly spaced multiples with a broad spread of beam, downlighting offers a good level of diffused lighting that is similar in shadow effect to light cloud at midday. For a more dramatic effect with sharp dark shadows similar to those of a spotlight use a single and narrow downlight beam. General downlighting in a bathroom is not a good idea as it creates shadows over the face, which is difficult for shaving and make-up. A downlight over the loo area, however, is particularly useful if you are partial to reading on the throne or a downlight directly over a bath makes you feel that you are bathing in light as well as water.

If the intention is to use the space for work or entertainment ensure that there is enough ambient light to fill the shadows. If you have the room height, pendant downlighters work well at reinforcing ambient light by creating pools of light over dining tables or work-surfaces as well as providing a focus to the room. The crystal chandelier is an extreme example of type.

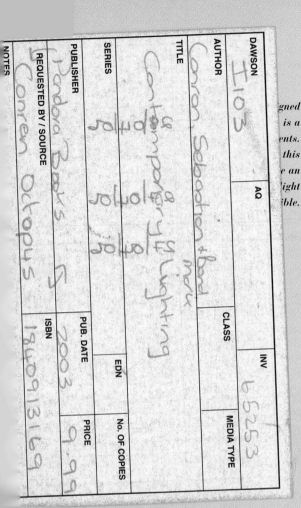

DAWSON			AQ		INV	
AUTHOR	Conran, Sebastian & Bond					
TITLE	Contemporary Lighting					
SERIES						
PUBLISHER	Pandora Books		PUB. DATE 2003		PRICE 9.99	
REQUESTED BY / SOURCE Conran Octopus			ISBN 1840913169			
NOTES						

H103 · 65253 · CLASS · MEDIA TYPE · EDN · No. OF COPIES

...gned is a ...ents. ...this ...e an ...light ...ible.

uplighting

Uplighting comes in many varieties and flavours, varying from wall-mounted sconces and adjustable-angle flood-lights to low-level floor wall-washers, table lamps and high-level standard lights. Low-level uplights tend to be especially effective when used in reception rooms and other areas. The absence of glare from the lamp is an important aspect of the received impression.

The fundamental principle of uplighting is to reflect the light off the walls or ceiling and into the room. This gives good indirect diffuse lighting, defining the parameters of the space with more interest than ceiling-mounted direct lighting. The really magical effect of uplighting is that it appears to lift the ceiling height by making the ceiling appear lighter and therefore further away. As such, it is quite perfect for low-ceilinged rooms and in spaces that you would like to appear larger.

The effect uplighters give is affected strongly by the colour and type of wall-covering that they are reflected off. Stripy wallpaper with vertical lines leads the eye upwards, creating space. In a narrow room, horizontal stripes widen the space by leading the eye along the wall. Combining lighting with these visual tricks adds to the illusion of more space. When lighting washes over walls, it is important that they are well finished or flat as the light highlights the tiniest of imperfections with oblique shadows. Conversely, this can be put to good use on textured walls, such as exposed brick-work, when it will accentuate the character of the surface.

Low-level uplighting also provides any room with warmth. Furniture lit from behind with uplighting can look dramatic as well as creating the impression of more space. Some table lamps can be an effective way to give uplighting in the middle of a room while offering an interesting sculptural accent to the environment.

Above *The Jill Wall, designed by King, Miranda and Arnaldi in 1978 for Flos. Here is a classic use of a double-ended halogen flood bulb housed so that most of the light is directed up while the cast glass fitting glows in the spillage. The design is also available as a floor-standing uplighter and the glass shade comes in medicine bottle blue, yellow, pink, white and green.*

Opposite *(background)* **and below** Luminator, *designed by Achille and Pier Giacomo Castiglioni in 1954 for Flos. This floor lamp uplighter was one of the first fittings designed around the integrated reflector mushroom spot lamp.*

Opposite *(foreground)* Atollo, *designed by Vico Magistretti in 1977 for Oluce and first made of lacquered aluminium. Since then it has been made from acrylic (1988) and Murano glass (1989). A geometric take on the classic table lamp, Atollo directs all light downwards onto the horizontal surface below.*

spot lighting

Spotlights derive from automotive headlamps and the full-scale versions that are used in theatres to create a small pool of light (or 'follow' spot) from the back of the auditorium on the stage to draw the audience's attention to a particular performer or action. They have a distinct advantage over other forms of directional lighting in that as they tend to be quite small for their output they can be easily mounted on ceilings or walls, and often they can be on freestanding pylons too. They generally work by using a parabolic reflector behind a light source to produce a parallel beam of light that does not diffuse over distance. Sometimes they are incorporated into the lamp itself. Lasers are the most extreme form of spotlight with a parallel beam angle of 0 degrees.

The average domestic spotlight is not nearly so narrowly focused, their main use is to project a well-defined, bright pool of light highlighting a particular area or object. These vary in intensity and geometry but generally they tend to be quite small and have a fairly narrow angle of beam compared to floodlights.

The consequential effect of spotlights is that their sharply defined dark shadows can be very dramatic, bleaching out any colour if there is not enough ambient light too: the eye assimilates to the darkness rather than the light. This makes them particularly good for highlighting objets d'art, sculptures or pictures at a distance from a ceiling or across a room. Spotlighting a picture from recessed lighting creates the illusion of more space. An entry hall or corridor is a good place for display, so spotlight objects and art here to create a portent to the contents of the rest of the home.

The kitchen is a treasure-trove of interesting objects that can be highlighted and picked out with single spotlights. Mundane pots and pans can be crown jewel-like decorative objects with selective lighting. Spots can also be usefully used to shoot pools of light on to central work surfaces, and in the bathroom, shoot spots on to baths and basins to see light dance on water. They can be put to good use as bedside lighting, too, as they can be aimed at pillows and are indispensable for reading in bed while not disturbing your partner.

Papiro, designed by Sergio Calatroni in 1988 for Pallucco Italia. With a flexible and directable adjustable floor lamp, the base, stem and diffuser are made from copper, natural colour and a nickel-chrome finish. Available in two heights, the lights are provided with an electronic transformer and dimmer with foot control lever. Unusually, this creates a pool of light by moving the light source close to the subject rather than projecting a narrow beam from a distance.

Non-drip paraffin wax candles can be an inexpensive and effective mood source if used in multiples, as here, making a feature of this disused fireplace. Be careful never to leave candles unattended.

candle lighting

These days we take it for granted that when we enter a dark room we can flick a switch and hey-presto we have light. But it was not always so. Our earliest ancestors would have first seen fire when lightning struck a tree. Soon man learned how to create, nurture and control fire himself, making torches, oil lamps and candles for convenient light sources after darkness – extending their useful day.

Today's decorative festive candles have their ancestry in what was once the principal source of artificial light – mutton-fat tallow candles for the poor and bees-wax for the rich and the church – we now use paraffin wax derived from crude oil. Then, with the advent of town gas in the early nineteenth century, efficient lamps were developed with the invention of the gas mantle, giving a far brighter, whiter light for both street and home.

Candles, however, have always been far more elegant and stylish than prosaic and economical oil

The warm glowing light of a candle is famously flattering if used in a table centre as it irons out chins and wrinkles. Used with abandon they give a wonderful character to a room in many evening circumstances.

lamps, especially if used in multiples. Today we rely on them more for atmosphere than for light. Characteristically, candles tend to give a very warm light with long, well-defined flickering shadows caused by their small light source. This is coupled with the diffuse glow of the wax, illuminated by the hungry flame that is soon to consume it.

Nightlights have the advantage of being comparatively inexpensive and lasting for a good eight hours. This makes them particularly useful as they can be lit early without the need to be serviced. They do need some help with their appearance, though. Naked they can look a little basic, but there are many specific lamp holders for them and they also give ample opportunities for improvisation.

Think safety, always be careful of fire. Think what will happen to them when they burn down low, be careful of nearby flammable objects and don't use wooden candle holders. Never leave a room for long with candles alight - especially to go to bed.

task lighting

Task lighting is created by floor or table lamps with cantilevered arms that can be easily adjusted so that the lamp throws a bright pool of light on to a zone of concentration for, say, reading or drawing. Typically, this light will be about five times the intensity required for the rest of the room.

Operating theatres are painted white for good reason. Not only does it aid hygiene but the white also reflects and optimizes a bright, even light throughout the space. There is also the familiar multi-headed (to avoid shadows) cluster of small spotlights suspended over the job in hand, creating an intensely bright pool of light on the area. This is an extreme but pertinent example of task lighting in action: the brighter the light, the smaller the pupils, so the more clearly the surgeon can see. The importance of good task lighting is often misunderstood or overlooked, especially in the home.

Task lighting's *raison d'être* comes down to the physics of biology. Put simply, when relaxed, the ideal eye is meant to focus in the middle distance. When looking around at objects near and far the eye has to work continually to adjust its focus to see clearly – the closer to, the harder the lens muscles have to work. Typically, when reading a newspaper, the focus can constantly be ranging from 30 to 60cm (12 to 24in), which can be quite strenuous to the eye, especially in poor light. The brighter the light intensity on the page, the smaller the iris can be contracted to let in the right level of light required to stimulate the retina. This, in turn, allows a wider depth of focus thereby reducing the amount of muscle activity needed to see clearly and subsequent tiredness. Simply put – the more light, the less tiring: hence the value of task lighting.

1 Archimoon Tech, *designed by Philippe Starck in 1998 for Flos. Used with a 35W low-voltage halogen capsule, his light has a similar articulated balance mechanism as the seminal Anglepoise (see page 17). The shade is available in various translucent colours.* **2 Tizio**, *designed by Richard Sapper in 1972 for Artemide. Here is a table lamp with double luminous intensity and revolving arms and head. It is made from painted metal and thermoplastic resin and the power supply is in the cylindrical base. The two cantilevered arms ingeniously conduct the 12V DC current to the capsule bulb. Tizio is also available with a useful floor stand.* **3 Archimoon Classic**, *again designed by Philippe Starck in 1998 for Flos, is similar to the Archimoon Tech shown alongside. This light has a conventional incandescent 60W lamp.* **4 Tolomeo**, *designed by de Lucchi and Fassina for Flos, has arms and a head that revolve in all directions. Made from polished and anodized aluminium, this utility styled light system comes in many different lamp fittings and forms including articulated wall-mounted, floor-standing and clamp heads.*

occasional lighting

There are certain lights that have such a conceptually extraordinary appearance that they cannot be easily categorized. Often weird and alien-looking, they can often seem like the domestic equivalent of pet UFOs. If furniture is to be likened to clothing for the home then some lights are surely the accessories and jewellery. Lights can be seen as functioning pieces of mechanical sculpture that add a highlight to any environment. The light-giver becomes an industrial art object or altarpiece of design and because lights are inherently bright, they attract attention to their physical forms as emitters of radiant energy. After the chair, the light is probably the next example of the designer's equivalent of the artist's self-portrait. Do not confuse these designer-ego-expression lights with the more functional architectural fittings whose aim is to provide usable light to a space. Oh no … the raison d'être here is to delight and stimulate – providing focus and interest to an environment.

Often very strong and dominating, these lights become modern treasures that have a history and personality that you can love and carry with you throughout your life.

These are not really lights as such, they are more ideas that happen to emit light. There has been probably more demonstration of conceptual ingenuity in the field of lighting than in any other area of environment related design. It is the eclectic mix of form with technological function that makes these lights the architectural equivalent of richly glittering jewels.

It is difficult to advise on how to use these objects as lighting as their output is so various in both quantity and quality. It is their actual appearance rather than their light to which they owe their existence, therefore they should be suitable to add interest to a dark corner or as a character to an otherwise lifeless room. Such occasional lights can also be a very useful means of adding colour to an otherwise monochromatic environment.

Sasso, designed by Caterina Fadda. More sculptural poetry than a conventional light source, the red glass 'pebble' only lights up when placed in contact with the metal strips on its perspex base.

material choices

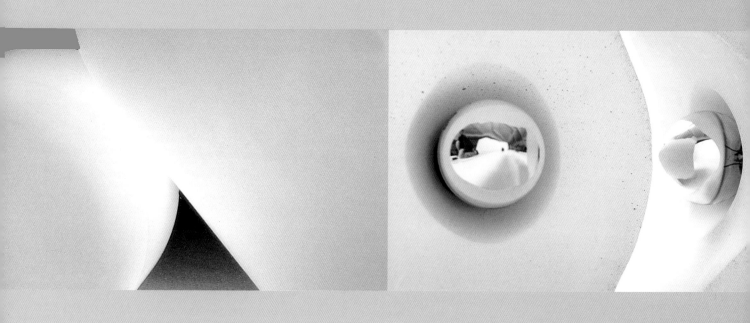

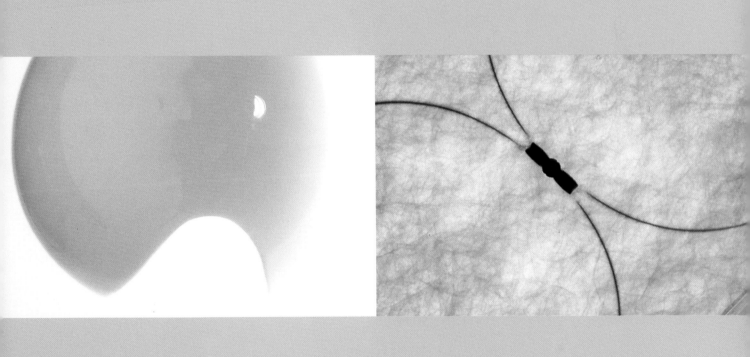

lights

It is important to have the right type of light for the right situation. A light suitable for a desk is different to that for a living room. Sometimes rooms also need to change their use throughout the day, in which case the lighting arrangement must be flexible too. Aim to achieve a balance between ambient light and glowing pools with perhaps accents of tightly focused point sources.

1 Taccia, *designed by Achille and Pier Giacomo Castiglioni in 1962 for Flos, gives an even light by reflecting the light off enamelled metal.* **2** Costanza, *designed by Paolo Rizzatto in 1986 for Luceplan (see also page 52).* **3** Pod Lens, *designed by Ross Lovegrove in 1998 for Luceplan. Made of injection-moulded polycarbonate, primarily this is an outdoor light as the material is resistant to ultraviolet rays, humidity, water and snow.* **4** Romeo Moon, *designed by Philippe Starck in 1998 for Flos. Available in glass or fabric shades, this table light is part of a system that offers coordinated lights for pendant, wall and floor.* **5** The pendant light *from the Terra Lighting Range designed by Pedro Silva Dias in 1997 for Proto Design. This small, ceramic pendant lamp is useful for providing accent lighting.* **6** Espiga Lamps, *designed by Sharon Bowles and Edgard Linares. Here are occasional floor lights designed to give some interesting shadow effects.* **7** Elvis, *designed by Charles Williams for Fontana Arte. The innovative way the crumpled translucent fabric is cast into the clear resin of the shade gives this angular table light an intriguing elegance.*

4

^
5 6

7
v

floor lights

Living rooms are the natural habitat of the floor lamp. Primarily used for social interaction, the light in these surroundings must be flattering to make people in them look as good as possible to each other. To create a warm atmosphere, it's best to try using a variety of different light sources at varying heights (remember low is flattering). To give a greater feeling of intimacy, emphasize pools of light around seating rather than having an even, bland light. Floor lamps are a good source of ambient light as is uplighting, especially if used at the side of the room reflecting light off the walls.

Bulky standard lamps in the middle of a room can cause clutter and take up space while admittedly emitting useful light so it's often a good idea to place them in corners, close to a wall, or at least out of walk-ways. Be wary of those with trip-over-able legs that stick out as well as those with topple-prone small bases (especially if you expect to have young children gallivanting about). Again, try to plan your lighting scheme to avoid trailing wires and cables, and have floor sockets installed if you wish to use lighting centrally in a room – you can never have too many sockets it seems.

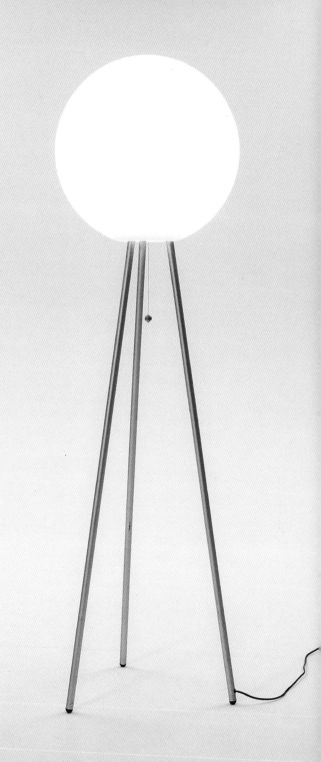

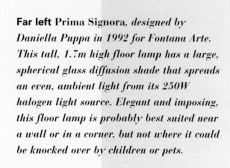

Far left Prima Signora, *designed by Daniella Puppa in 1992 for Fontana Arte. This tall, 1.7m high floor lamp has a large, spherical glass diffusion shade that spreads an even, ambient light from its 250W halogen light source. Elegant and imposing, this floor lamp is probably best suited near a wall or in a corner, but not where it could be knocked over by children or pets.*

Left Eclipse 3, *designed by Peter Wylly in 1996 for Babylon Design. The lamp shade of this floor lamp is made from biodegradable polystyrene sheets cut and formed into three layers. The support and base are created from mild steel. This futuristic piece is rather less likely to suffer expensive damage as it is not so top heavy and has a light-weight plastic diffuser.*

Right Toio, *designed by Achille and Pier Giacomo Castiglioni for Flos. This floor lamp gives direct light that is adjustable in height on its enamelled steel base and nickel-plated brass stem. This classic light was one of the first domestic lights to use low-voltage tungsten-halogen lumps as developed for the automotive industry.*

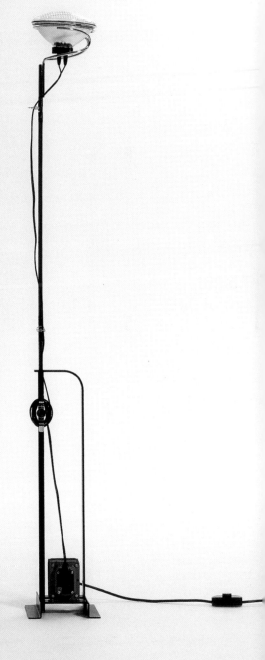

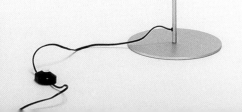

1 Gilda, *designed by Enrico Franzolini in 1997 for Pallucco Italia, has a large lamp shade made from synthetic parchment paper.*
2 Lowlight and Highlight Lamps, *designed by Helene Tiedemann for David Design. These cute lamps have a quirky animal-like character, which is more witty than jokey.* **3 Iride**, *designed by Pierluigi Nicolin for Artemide. Remote-controlled, each light gives off a different colour which can be varied according to mood.* **4 Lola**, *designed by Alberto Meda and Paolo Rizzatto in 1987 for Luceplan. With its swivelling head, micro-perforated metal reflector, telescopic stem in carbon fibre and die-cast articulated tripod, this sci-fi-looking piece uses racing car technology with appropriate wishbone styling.* **5 Helice**, *designed by Marc Newson in 1993 for Flos. In contrast, this floor-standing lamp with halogen flood has a more 1950s sci-fi reference. Subtle and successful coloured lighting effects are obtained using glass filters.* **6 Lucilla**, *designed by Paolo Rizzatto in 1994 for Luceplan, is available in a small and table version, and also as a pendant lamp. The hanging shade fabric is a non-combustible fabric that is similar to that used to weave the suits worn by astronauts.* **7** *This chandelier-like construction produced by Artemide has coloured glass organic shapes suspended from a metal hoop.*

2

3

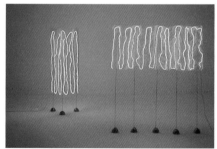

1

1 **Long Wave, Short Wave,** *designed by Bianchini Graelik Rozenberg in 1997 for Pallucco Italia, is a maleable, free-standing art light with a vibrant green-blue tone optic-fibre that emits a soft light source.* 2 **Globlow Floor Lamp 01** *(shown inflated and deflated), designed by Vesa Hinkola, Markus Nevalainen and Rane Vaskivuori for Valvomo Design. When switched on, this ingenious floor lamp inflates via a motorized fan and continues to gently cycle between its inflated and deflated states – the effect is surprisingly serene.*
3 **Papiro,** *designed by Sergio Calatroni in 1997 for Pallucco Italia. This is an adjustable floor lamp with a base, stem and diffuser made in copper, available in natural colour and nickel-chrome finish and in two sizes.*

Low lighting reflected off walls tends to flatter and give warmth to a space. In addition, small low and glowing lights can usefully add localized pools of colour that do not spill out into the rest of the space, and add interest day or night. Low-level uplighters can be used to good effect positioned behind sofas and other furniture, creating a greater sense of space. Lights that give off strongly patterned light particularly need to be placed close to walls so that their play of shadows is not lost.

Living rooms are ideal places for featuring floor lights as interesting sculptural objects in themselves, especially those whose light output is fairly vestigial. These light-emitting, sometimes alien-looking objects really can make quite a dramatic focal point to a room. Another idea is to occasionally swap around lights within the home as this can give quite a sense of change without affecting the ways in which the rooms are used.

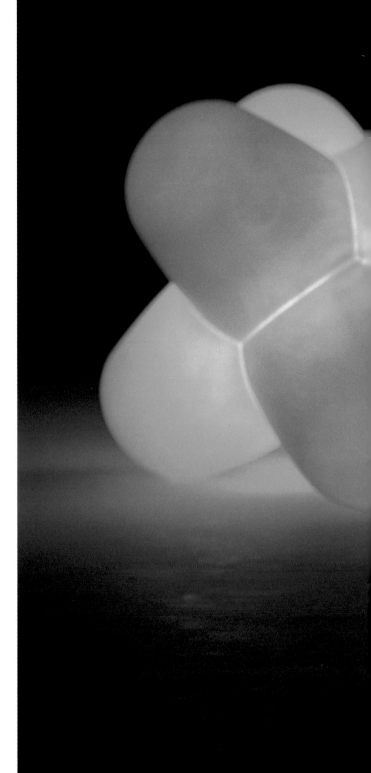

Jack Light, designed by Tom Dixon in 1996 for Eurolounge. Inspired by the children's game of jacks, these versatile light-emitting modules can be used in a variety of ways from stools to table bases, they can also be stacked vertically. They are made from rotationally moulded polyethylene and made in a range of colours.

Clockwise from bottom left Havana, *designed by Jozeph Forakis in 1993 for Foscarini, features four plastic diffusers suspended from each other by small metal rings. Orbital Terra, designed by Ferruccio Laviani in 1992 for Foscarini. The light from this collection of amorphous coloured glass shapes that are arranged up a steel spine frame is emitted from 40W 'golf ball' lamps. Less flamboyantly, it is also available in just white opal glass and individually as wall-mounted lights. Luminator, designed by Achille and Pier Giacomo Castiglioni in 1954 for Flos, as shown in its full glory (see page 30). Tube, designed by Christian Deuber in 1997 for Pallucco Italia. Here is a fluorescent tube-based floor lamp with an acrylic diffuser and metal support cradle base. It can be moved away from the base unit for a distance of up to 4m and leaned against another piece of furniture, a wall, or just laid on the floor. 2198, first produced by Fontana Arte in 1954, is a crisply styled piece of purist design using natural cherry with turned aluminium fittings topped by an opalescent glass shade.*

Spiral Light, designed by Tom Dixon in 1992. This tapering helix of gold- or silver-leafed mild steel with integrated dichroic uplighter is a simple and intriguing form that gives off dramatic shadows on nearby walls and ceilings. It looks almost as good switched off as on.

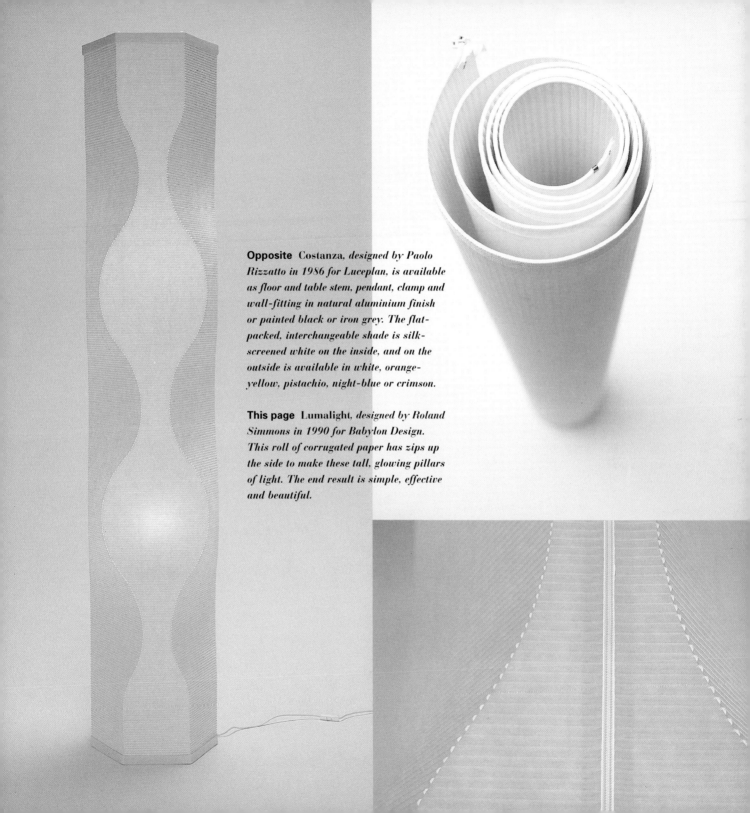

Opposite Costanza, *designed by Paolo Rizzatto in 1986 for Luceplan, is available as floor and table stem, pendant, clamp and wall-fitting in natural aluminium finish or painted black or iron grey. The flat-packed, interchangeable shade is silk-screened white on the inside, and on the outside is available in white, orange-yellow, pistachio, night-blue or crimson.*

This page Lumalight, *designed by Roland Simmons in 1990 for Babylon Design. This roll of corrugated paper has zips up the side to make these tall, glowing pillars of light. The end result is simple, effective and beautiful.*

table lights

Below left Glo-Ball, *designed by Jasper Morrison in 1998 for Flos. Shaped more like a tangerine than an orange, here is another super-minimalist creation from an international design supernova.*

Below right Filo Table, *designed by Peter Christian in 1994 for Aktiva. The swivelling polycarbonate shade directs light usefully and is available in several colours: white, orange, green and purple. The metal base and fittings are silver powder coated.*

Opposite left to right 2198 TA, *first produced by Fontana Arte in 1954 (see also page 50, bottom right). Ilos, designed by Pearson Lloyd in 1998 for Classicon. Available in three sizes, the light has a blown glass shade with ground ribbed glass diffuser below. Miss Sissi, designed by Philippe Starck in 1991 for Flos. This miniature table lamp is made in brightly coloured, beautifully moulded plastic. It is both inexpensive and useful giving direct light up and down and some coloured diffused light to the side. On Off, designed by A. Meda, F. Raggi and D. Santachiara in 1988 for Luceplan. On Off is turned on and off by altering the position of its balance. The thermoplastic polyurethane makes this little glowing mouse safe to manipulate.*

It helps to think of some lights as large vases with bunches of flowers that can be scattered around the room radiating warm light and bonhomie, or else view them as witty little table-top sculptural statements. Designer-object-lights abound and are therefore what immediately spring to mind in this category. Subtle humour is often a key component in these designs, giving them character and humanity – but remember the dictum 'witty not jokey, for a joke is only ever funny once'. Having some plastic dinosaur with a candle bulb protruding from its mouth may amuse for a day or two; but how long will it be before it lights the cupboard under the stairs?

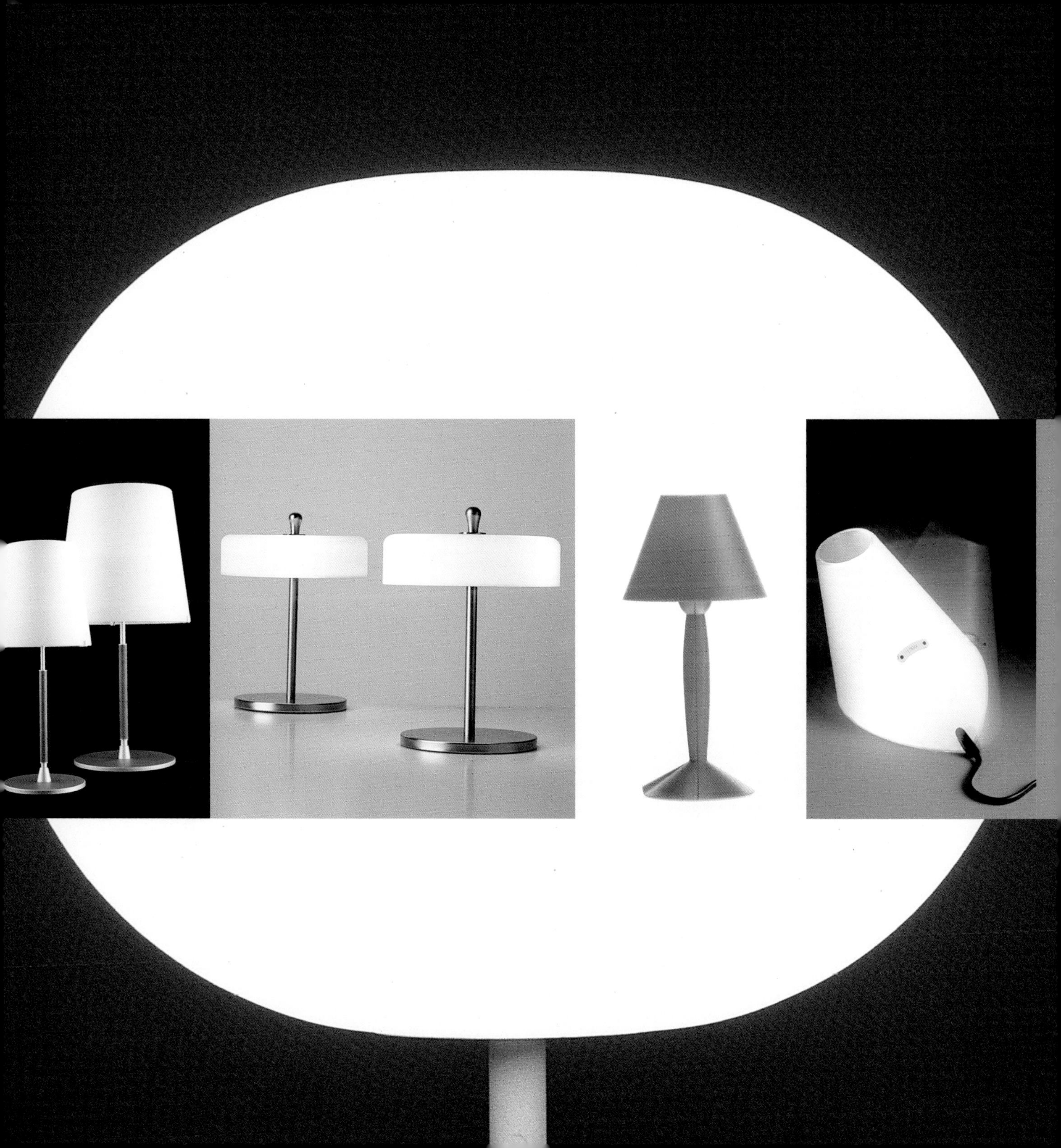

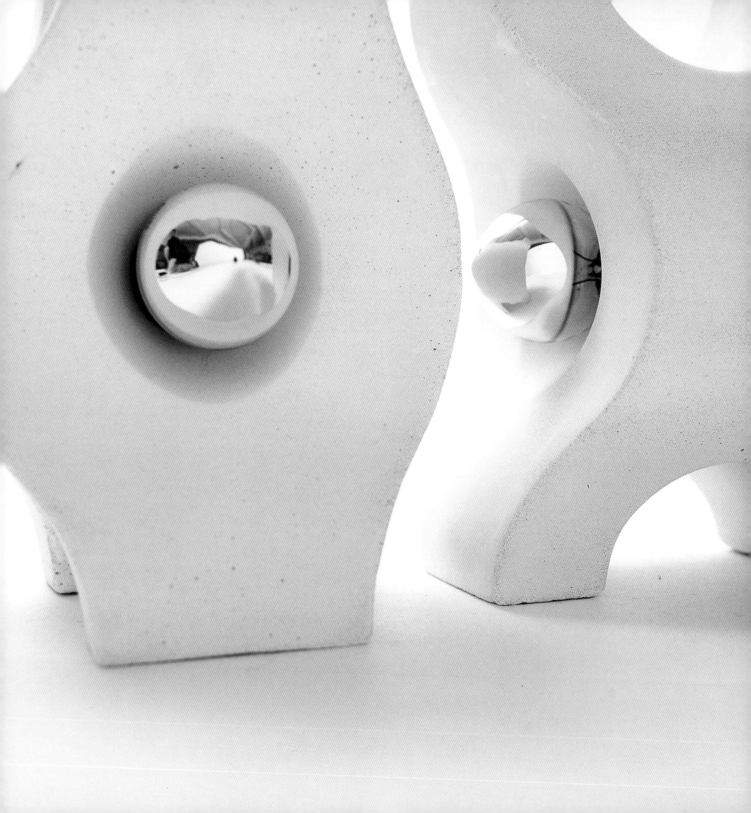

Intriguingly, there has been recent interest in ingenious lights using slip-cast ceramic technology intrinsic to the manufacture of lavatory bowls. They have become popular with some of the more intrepid, intuitive, independent designers, but how useful they are and how long they will be in vogue remains to be seen. They are, however, quite beautiful having a sort of Marcel Duchamp's 'found art' quality to them. This reference to the famous Dada art movement of the 1920s is quite deliberate and is evident in many great luminary designers' work including Achille Castiglioni (see pages 112-13) and Ingo Maurer (see pages 114-15).

Traditional takes on short-stem standard lamps with semi-opaque shades continue to work successfully – proving the concept. The shades provide a very useful control of light (especially when used with dimmers),

Left and above *Oxo Light, designed by Peter Wylly in 1997 for Babylon Design. Made in cement, when stacked, these forms are clearly inspired by the shape of the Lumalight column on page 53.*

Top right Table lamp *from the* Terra Lighting Range *designed by Konstantin Gricic in 1997 for Proto Design. This ceramic form is apparently inspired by the 'Wee Willie Winkie' candle holder.*

Right Lightbowl 1,2, *designed by Sophie Chandler for Alternative Light. This floor/table lamp uses the aesthetic qualities of classic light bulbs resting in a glass bowl with only one switched on to create an intriguing glowing sculpture.*

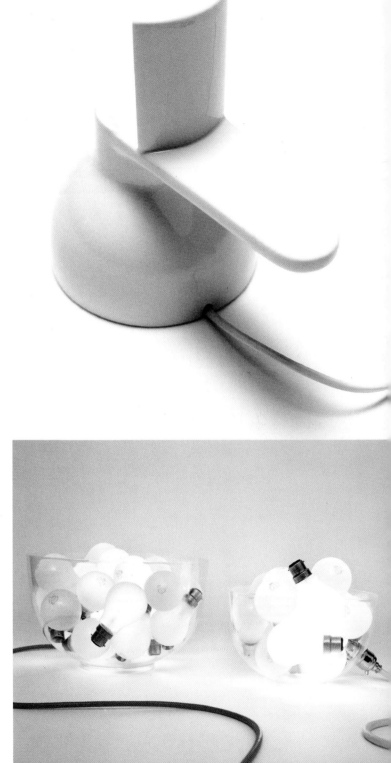

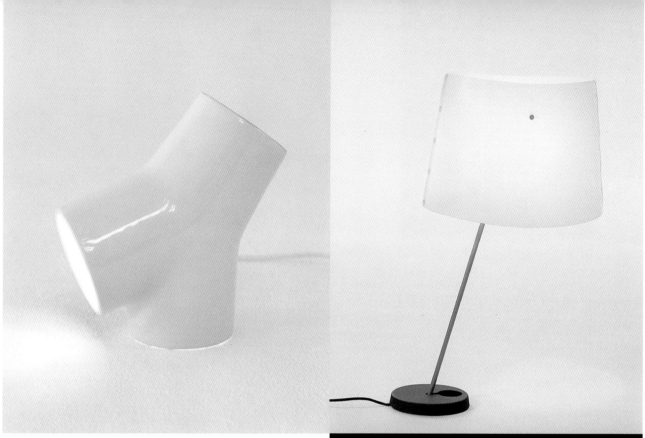

Above and opposite T13 *from the* Terra Lighting Range *designed by Sebastian Bergne in 1997 for Proto Design. This slip-cast ceramic form can be used in several ways, ranging from a table lamp to a pendant fitting.*

Top right Twist & Light 1, *designed by Sebastian Bergne in 1996 for Driade, is a table lamp with tilting aluminium grey painted stem, white polystyrene shade and cast iron base, painted dark grey. The light is also available as a floor light with a longer stem.*

Right *The heat from this lamp, designed by Shiu-Kay Kan, rises and passes through small turbine blades causing the patterned inner filter to rotate. Amusing for children, but it is quite delicate.*

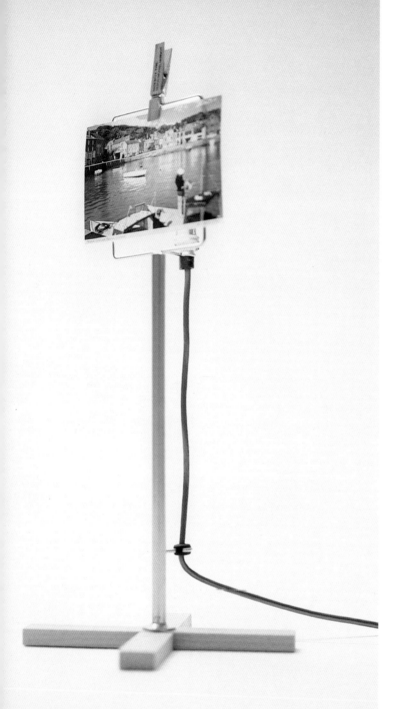

obscuring the primary light source while shafting the light up to reflect off the ceiling and washing it down to pool on a horizontal surface.

Glowing table lights can also be used to provide useful diffuse ambient light to a room, although again it is best if they are used at the edge of a room so that some of their light is reflected back. In this case they can, to some extent, counteract the colouring effect often found if you use wall-washers with coloured walls.

Left Postcard Light, *designed by Michael Marriott, is a steel tube postcard with a wooden clothes peg and wire frame.*

Above Shogun Tavolo, *designed by Mario Botta in 1986 for Artemide. Here is a table lamp with perforated, sheet-metal, revolving diffusers that refer to the cylindrical forms found in Botta's architecture. It is painted white and black and gives a wonderful play on shadows and light.*

Left Fibre Space, *manufactured by Mathmos, has a perforated shade on an aluminium base. The fountain of light emits from a revolving fibre optic.*

Lio, *designed by Sebastian Bergne for Driade. Here is a slab-sided table lamp with a white blow-moulded polypropylene shade. It is a simple piece of minimalist sculpture.*

Again, the position in the room and height at which they are placed will have a profound effect on the quality of light they provide.

Table lamps are versatile but they do need tables or other horizontal surfaces, which can make them inflexible to use. It's good to position them near windows so that the light pattern does not change too much with nightfall and always try to position them so that their bulbs are not visible, both when standing and sitting. Importantly, avoid trailing flexes and cables – they are not only unsightly but also particularly dangerous if tripped over and a mass of ceramic, glass and white hot metal arcs through the room.

Finally, although their primary function is to provide light, some table lamps are so inept at this that their function becomes one of a decorative object. However, this is clearly a major part of their agenda too. The once reviled but now revered *Lava lamp* is an excellent case-in-point.

Opposite Solo Table Light, *designed by Douglas Bryden, Richard Smith and Stephen Young in 1998 for the Arkitype Design Partnership. This table lamp comes as a polypropylene flat-pack ready for self-assembly. It is a simple and inexpensive way to make a fun light.*

Left Jet, *manufactured by Mathmos in 1999, is made from melamine, spun aluminium and glass. The heat from the lamp causes the coloured liquid to blob about in a colourless fluid. Once reviled but now revered, this is probably the most sophisticated contemporary version of the generically labelled lava lamp.*

desk
lights

Traditionally, the primary criterion for desk lamps is that they should be good for reading and writing by. However, the proliferation of computers has meant that there is also the additional requirement of providing shadow-free ambient light for the keyboard and to counteract the glare of the screen which otherwise can be quite tiring. Again, the physical mechanism is to reduce the pupil size, increasing usable focal distance. It is useful to position these lamps next to any seating where you may want to read or next to a telephone where you might need to take messages. They can also be used to provide localized spotlighting, such as pools of light for floral displays or 'art objects'.

These lights need to be practical and easily adjustable, and good examples are the seminal *Anglepoise* (see page 17) and Richard Sapper's equally innovative *Tizio* (also see page 17). The *Tizio* heralded the introduction of the tiny, cool, quartz-halogen capsule lamps that benefited this genre of lights by producing small lamp heads. These don't get in the way and allow a lighter, more elegant structure to be designed. The hi-tech mechanical articulation inherent in these lights

Berenice, designed by Paolo Rizzatto and Alberto Meda in 1985 for Luceplan. This lightweight insect-like form is one of the most beautiful desk lamps of the genre. Made from die-cast aluminium and stiffened nylon, the pressed glass reflector has an enamelled white interior and anti-UV protection glass.

often gives them an insect-like lightness similar to a grasshopper or dragonfly. They can also have the feel of miniature tower-cranes, fire trucks or cherry pickers (I wonder how long will it be before we see someone design one using just such a toy for the mechanism?).

Bedside tables are another habitat for desk lamps. Bedrooms must feel inviting and a key to feeling cosy is switchable lighting very close to the bed. Bedside lamps can be aimed at pillows and are indispensable for reading in bed. Whether wall- or table-mounted, lamps with cantilevered arms can be easily adjusted to move the lamp head over the bed head, throwing a bright pool of light on the page.

Below left *Fortebraccio, designed by Alberto Meda and Paolo Rizzatto in 1998 for Luceplan. The chic-cum-macho cantilever mechanism used here appears to be a celebration of precision engineering. It is finished in black, metal, yellow or red.*

Below *Ray, designed by Caputo and Power in 1996 for Fontana Arte. The lamp shade on this table lamp is suspiciously flower-pot like.*

Opposite *AJ, designed by Arne Jacobsen in 1960 for Louis Poulsen. A classic from a design guru, the shade of this luminaire can be pivoted vertically. The table light has a push button switch in the base, while the floor light has a foot switch.*

ceiling lights

The chandelier is the queen of all pendant lighting. Used in great halls, the point sources of the candles are enhanced with high refraction cut crystal which teases apart the spectrographic components of candle light into iridescent blues, yellows and reds, producing a rich glittering effect. The candelabra bereft of crystal comes next in the social pecking order, elegantly giving a good light to feast by. They are akin to a floating sculpture radiating from the centre of a space.

Pendant lights, so popular in the 50s and 60s, have recently and perhaps not surprisingly enjoyed a revival. Depending on their design, they can often combine the virtuous effects of both uplights and downlights in various proportions. Unfortunately, they can emphasize some of the less desirable vices too. Sometimes practicality can give sway to the preferences of fashion; and life would be pretty boring if it didn't!

Uplighting lifts a ceiling, making the ceiling appear lighter and further away, giving the illusion of more space. However, compared to uplighters, the shadow a pendant casts will be bigger, sharper and darker. Beware of pendant lights, because, unless used carefully, they can be a disastrous mistake – especially in smallish bedrooms and living rooms. Too close to the ceiling looks mean, too low means you bang your head! They are undoubtedly at their most effective when used in multiples to light large spaces.

Star, designed by Tom Dixon in 1997 for Eurolounge. This striking pendant light can also be used as a table or floor lamp. It was allegedly inspired by styrofoam cups stuck to a child's football and was manufactured from rotationally moulded polyethylene available in a selection of colours.

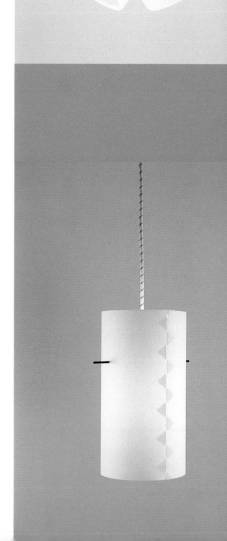

Right Pendant *and* table lamp *from the* Terra Lighting
Range, *designed by Sebastian Bergne in 1997 for Proto Design.
More slip-cast ceramic forms (see pages 58-9).*

Below Paper Pendant, *designed by Nazanin Kamali for Aero.
This cylindrical pendant shade in white with a mild steel
frame in silver or black has a simple shape with neat joining
detail and cable. It also packs flat.*

Overleaf Fucsia, *designed by Achille Castiglioni in 1996 for
Flos. This cluster of glass cones is a modern interpretation of
the chandelier but even more serene and beautiful. As shown, it
is available in several groupings and configurations.*

Remember that if you hang anything from the wall or
ceiling it gives the illusion of making the room seem
smaller, so make sure that you have sufficient ceiling
height before committing to your purchase. The
situations where these types of light work best are high
hallways and over dining tables where they light the
food better than the people eating it – this is somewhat
alleviated when used in multiple batteries. Again, for
this reason, pendant lights do not make a very good
light for living rooms.

Small hanging pendant lights with translucent
shades can be usefully used above work surfaces
producing beneficial small pools of light to work under.
However, it is vital that they are positioned so that they
don't create shadows or produce glare. The kitchen is
also an area where ceiling lights are used quite
frequently, often with good effect. However, do consider
what the lamps will look like with a gentle film of grease
on them – so don't situate them near your hob, especially
if they are going to be a pain to clean (often this is not
possible either) – a dusty, greasy pendant is a
mieserable sight.

Top left Cina, *designed by Rodolfo Dordoni in 1994 for Flos. The moulded glass shades are reminiscent of traditional Japanese paper lanterns and use conventional 150W bulbs.* **Top right** Anywhere Light, *produced by Aero. Here, a spun aluminium, bobbin-shaped shade spreads light up and down.* **Bottom left** Daisy, *made from polypropylene and also available as a floor-standing light, was designed by Roy Sant.* **Bottom right** *The shade of this Filo Pendant, designed by Peter Christian in 1994 for Aktiva, is made from polycarbonate in white, orange, green and purple (see also page 54).*

Opposite top left UFO, *designed by Nick Crosbie for Inflate. This pendant light is inflatable and made from vacuum formed PVC.*

Top right UFL, *designed by Peter Wylly in 1998 for Babylon Design. Here is a multi-coloured pendant light made from aluminium with polypropylene: the coloured filters give off a warmly coloured glow.*

Bottom left Alzaia, *designed by Vico Magistretti in 1996 for Fontana Arte. This large (it has a diameter of 50cm/20in) but elegant pendant shade with diffused glass lamp holder houses a hefty 150W conventional incandescent bulb.*

Bottom right Zuuk, *designed by Ingo Maurer in 1994, has a stainless steel, colourless, heat-resistant, satin-frosted glass halogen bulb. It comes complete with a surface-mounted ceiling fixture and anodized base-plate cover.*

The general effect of downlighting is that of visually dropping a ceiling – because the ceiling is in shadow it therefore appears to come closer to the viewer. Whether track-mounted or recessed, ceiling lights are especially effectual in halls and corridors as they downlight the floor and pathway. They also can be usefully angled as wall-washer floods or spotlights for pictures and architectural features. If used as wall-washers they provide effective curtains of light, too. Positioned carefully over seating they can also provide a usefully bright light to read books and magazines by.

Above Light Light, *designed by Clementine Hope. These flat-pack plastic images of a chandelier on a shade have been screen printed on semi-opaque plastic panels with a water-based ink. Available in white or grey, the plastic panels slot together to form a cube-shaped lamp shade that readily attaches to a pendant light bulb holder.*

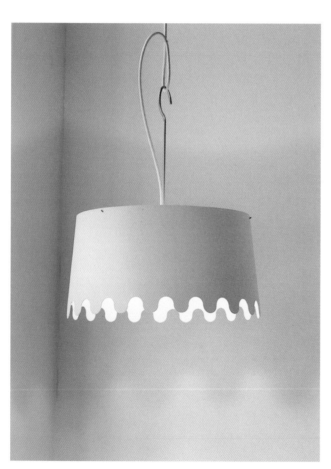

Left Waves, *designed by Johannes Norlander in 1998 for Box. The opaque shade with its large diameter and stubby fingers gives an effect curiously like an upside-down splash of milk. Note the adjustable coat hanger hook detail above the shade.*

Right and opposite Saturn Lamp, *produced in 1999 by Jam. The housing of this lamp is formed using closed cell Zotefoam and an Ecotone bulb, which infuses the translucent foam with a brightly coloured soft organic light.*

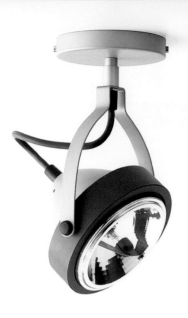

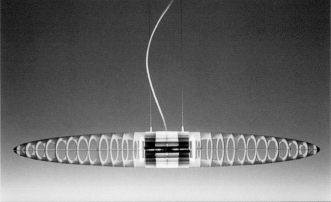

Above Search Light SL-111, *designed by the in-house team at Akitva in 1994. Track or ceiling mounted and finished in silver, white, black special or polished aluminium, the cap on the capsule bulb ensures that spillage is minimized and the light is focused in the direction intended.*

Top right Titania, *designed by Alberto Meda and Paolo Rizzatto in 1995 for Luceplan, featuring a lamellar shell in natural aluminium. Five pairs of interchangeable polycarbonate filters, silk screened in green, red, blue, yellow and violet, determine the different colourings of the shell while still continuing to emit a white light. Redolent of a skinless air-frame, the skeletal structure has an eerie UFO-like presence.*

Right Romeo Moon S2, *designed by Philippe Starck in 1998 for Flos. With moulded glass or fabric shades, this pendant light is part of a system that offers co-ordinated lights for table, wall and floor use. A semi-industrial looking object, it has been house-tamed for domestic use.*

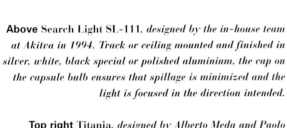

Above Clio, Erato, Urania, Musa sospensione, *designed by Rodolfo Dordoni in 1994 for Artemide. Suspension lamps with double on/off switching and two- or three-coloured glass diffusers are available in many different versions utilizing the components in different configurations.*

Right Don't run we are your friends, *designed by Roberto Feo for El Ultimo Grito. Adjustable pendant lights, made of acrylic plastic, the thin connecting wires coming from the tip of each shade are passed over ceiling-mounted eyelets giving a seesaw effect to the deliberately UFO-looking lights.*

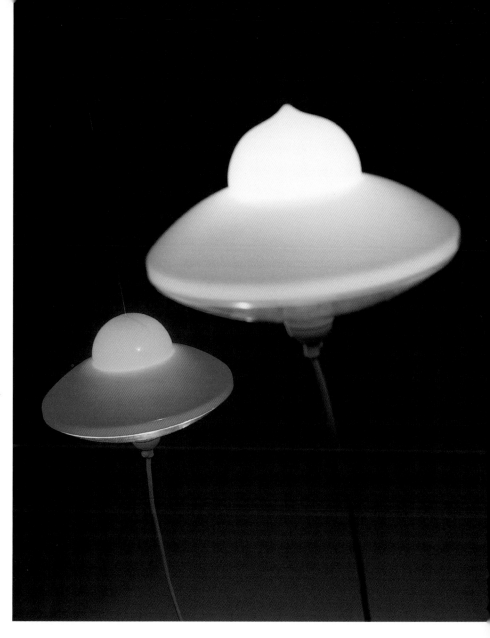

Glo-Ball Pendant, *designed by Jasper Morrison in 1998 for Flos. Shaped more like a tangerine than an orange, this ceiling light is designed in the spirit of being minimalist.*

of little conical lights with a high-tech appearance. Such track lighting systems are particularly useful for highlighting pictures.

Below Medea, Erilo Chronocolour series, *manufactured by Artemide. These semi-recessed 12V dichroic lamps have transformers housed in the ceiling void and use small coloured diffusers to add interest more than to reduce light spillage and glare.*

Opposite left PH Snowball, *designed by Poul Henningsen in 1958 for Louis Poulsen. This height-adjustable pendant uses a series of curved metal screens. The inside is matt and the outside high-gloss white finish screen to give an evenly focused diffused light.*

Below Ya Ya Ho, *designed by Ingo Maurer and team for his own company, is a low-voltage lighting system fed by a transformer to reduce the mains current. It seems to have been inspired by the overhead power cables found in many European tram systems.*

Top right Mikado Track, *designed by F.A. Porsche for Artemide. This ceiling- and wall-mounted track light system has a series*

Opposite right Satellite Pendant, *designed by Vilhelm Wohlert in 1959 for Louis Poulsen. This onion-shaped opal glass dome is open to the underside to produce an overall glow.*

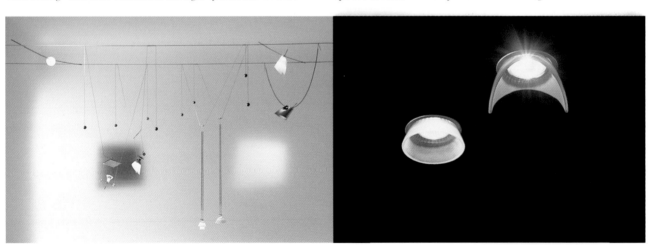

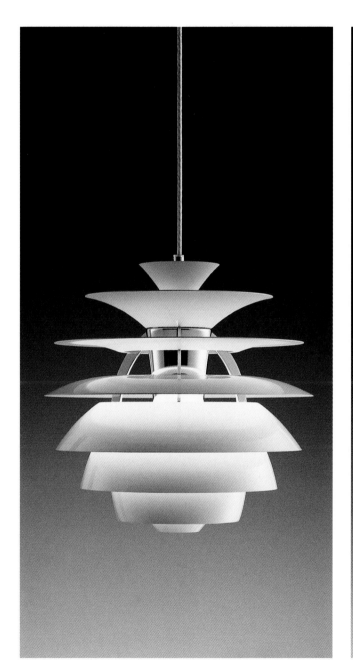

The general effect of downlighting is that of visually dropping a ceiling – because the ceiling is in shadow it therefore appears to come closer to the viewer.

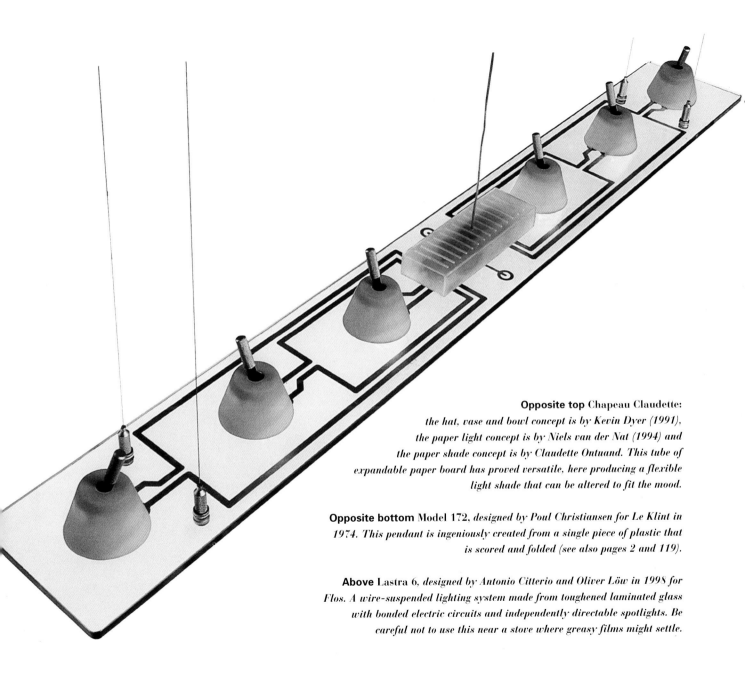

Opposite top Chapeau Claudette:
the hat, vase and bowl concept is by Kevin Dyer (1991),
the paper light concept is by Niels van der Nat (1994) and
the paper shade concept is by Claudette Ontuand. This tube of
expandable paper board has proved versatile, here producing a flexible
light shade that can be altered to fit the mood.

Opposite bottom Model 172, *designed by Poul Christiansen for Le Klint in*
1974. This pendant is ingeniously created from a single piece of plastic that
is scored and folded (see also pages 2 and 119).

Above Lastra 6, *designed by Antonio Citterio and Oliver Löw in 1998 for*
Flos. A wire-suspended lighting system made from toughened laminated glass
with bonded electric circuits and independently directable spotlights. Be
careful not to use this near a stove where greasy films might settle.

wall lights

Historically, wall lights stem from the days when flickering, flaming torches were de rigueur, attached to the wall with wrought iron fittings. But with the advent of candles and more delicate oil lamps they lost favour a little – at least until the advent of town gas in the nineteenth century, which had to be on the wall when this form of lighting became particularly popular once again. Recently, the trend has been not only to use them to provide direct light but also to act as floodlights reflecting light off the ceiling into rooms. This has been particularly successful with the advent of lower ceilings in contemporary environments.

Ariette, designed by Tobia Scarpa in 1973 for Flos. This kite-shaped wall or ceiling lamp gives diffused light, housed in fire-resistant synthetic fabric stretched over a sprung framework. It is available in three sizes and uses a gang of four 40W incandescent golf ball lights.

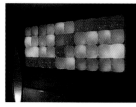

Left and right Chromawall, *designed by Jeremy Lord for the Colour Light Co. Chromawall is a modular, wall-mounted colour changing light display system. Each module radiates light that changes colour slowly and smoothly. There are no moving parts and the changes are controlled electronically as different coloured lamps are dimmed up and down. Each module contains four colour change cells, which each include four specially coloured filament lamps.*

Below left Wall A Wall A, *designed by Philippe Starck in 1993 for Flos. This is a diffused wall lamp with a coloured wall bracket and a milky white plastic diffuser with coloured filters. Its ingenious press switch gently glows when the light is off.*

Below right Train Train, *designed by Marc Sadler in 1996 for Flos. The ability to evenly light the face makes this flexible modular light system perfect for a mirror surround. It also incorporates a mains output for razors and toothbrushes.*

Opposite, clockwise from top left Drop 2, *designed by Marc Sadler in 1993 for Flos. The lamp cover is moulded in a transluscent flexible compound. The base is a rigid transluscent plastic which gives a coloured glowing halo.* Icon 'Holes', *designed by Peter Christian in 1996 for Aktiva. It has a screen-printed image and an anodized aluminium frame that comes with several different patterns and in various panel sizes.* Lola Wall, *designed by Alberto Meda and Paolo Rizzatto in 1987 for Luceplan. With a swivelling carbonfibre head, micro-perforated metal reflector, up to 250W halogen and protection glass, this organic-looking piece uses advanced technology. The general directional light is controlled by moving the small protruding rod.* Searchlight, *designed by the in-house team at Aktiva in 1996. A wall-mounted uplighter available in two versions and different finishes – silver, white or black or polished aluminium.*

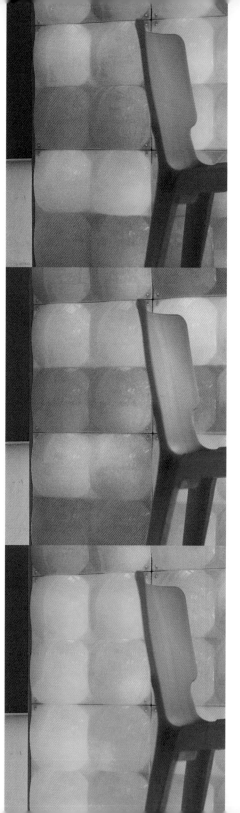

There are generally three types of wall lighting – floods, which cast light back on to the wall or ceiling; glowing, which emit a diffused light directly into a space (or a combination of the two), and spotlights, which project bright, tight pools of light with sharp shadows. An entry hall is a place for display and the natural habitat of wall lights as they are off the floor and out of the way. In addition to providing a cosy greeting, wall-mounted lights provide a dramatic focal point to a smallish space. The lighting level should generally be fairly subdued in preparation for entering the actual living spaces but make sure that there is adequate light on the floor for a feeling of welcome and security.

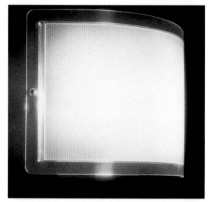

Top left Circus Grande, *designed by Defne Koz in 1994 for Foscarini. The large convex bun-shaped plastic moulding stands slightly away from the surface to give good ambient light. This light is available in two sizes, and can be used equally well on the wall or the ceiling.*

Centre left Screen, *designed by Alberto Meda and Paolo Rizzatto in 1989 for Luceplan. This is an injection-moulded acrylic screen with a white silk-screened prismatic surface. It is available in two sizes and works particularly well near mirrors where the large area of even light is especially effective.*

Left Acheo Wall, *designed by Gianfranco Frattini in 1989 for Artemide. This techy-looking painted metal and Pyrex glass flood light comes with various wall and ceiling fittings.*

Zero One, *designed by Ingo Maurer and team in 1990 for his own company. A white Corian body with frosted mirror supports a protective glass cover that surrounds a halogen bulb. The light from this brick-sized light can be simply adjusted by moving the reflecting, diffusing mirror along the wire support.*

Rubber Light, *designed by Mark Bond in 1998 for Bond Projects. The heat-proof elastomeric sheath/shade pulls firmly over the light bulb that then nonchalantly hangs from a wooden peg, which is in turn screwed into a wall.*

outdoor lights

Fire and particularly fireworks provide the most dramatic and spiritual forms of outdoor light. There are many tools for outdoor lighting: floodlights, pendants off trees, twinkle bulbs and firelight – but the greatest of these is always flame. There is little to beat the romance and carefree atmosphere of warm summer evenings when the sun sets quickly. This reverie can be usefully prolonged with some sensitive and imaginative exterior lighting. The important thing, however, is to avoid the glaring football pitch flood-lit approach.

Wisdom has it that there are two basic types of outdoor lighting: plant light and moonlight. Lights hidden in plants make them glow with a mysterious luminescence. Unfortunately, this is no help to general navigation in the dark for which you need some downlights – as high as possible – to bathe a lawn or terrace. Alternatively, there are bulkhead lights and the waist-level guiding lights favoured by municipal walkways, but more elegant and miniature ones are available for domestic use.

A more romantic approach is to line paths with the long-lasting nightlight candles in wind-proof glass holders These can be simply made by placing a nightlight candle in a glass tumbler inside a white paper bag – the effect is quite magical: almost like an aircraft runway for the fairies.

Left *In sparklers, steel filings are mixed with an oxidizing agent such as potassium perchlorate and combined with gum arabic. When lit, the mixture spectacularly oxidizes in the way a lamp filament would do if it were not protected from oxygen by a vacuum.*

Right *Jack Light, designed by Tom Dixon in 1996 for Eurolounge. Available in a range of colours, these rotationally moulded (like traffic cones) polyethylene light-emitting nodules can be used in a variety of ways from stools to table bases. They can also be stacked and are suitable for occasional outside use.*

The urban environment has become a miasma of light which although brash and exciting also means that the stars are completely obliterated. The reality of modern-day Tokyo also eclipses the portrayal of the urban future as seen in Ridley Scott's movie Blade Runner.

Domestically, outside lighting tends to be used only infrequently for jovial entertaining and on special occasions. This gives the daring opportunity to be quite radical and theatrical, using coloured floodlighting and spots. Alternatively, there is the tasteful, romantic approach with soft, glowing, subdued areas to balance out the brash. Whatever, it's a wonderful fact that with a little imagination and daring the most dreary yard or garden by day can become the fantasy of your choice by night. Keep the lights low to guide and use lots of colour, with accents of flame and candle.

Architectural details can be dramatically enhanced and revealed with the use of both spotlights and floodlights. Water will always be enchantingly respondent to some well-focused spotlights. Don't kill the mystery of darkness, though. Rather, be theatrical, using pools and little twinkly bright bits. Christmas tree lights work wonderfully in summer evenings, strung through the odd bush or just lighting the edge of the path. Also, think candles, candles, candles. Enough is not a word they understand, but they are a bit like daffodils as they work best in clusters.

Opposite left Pantarei 300 Halflight, *manufactured by Artemide. This exterior bulkhead light can be mounted so that the lamp illuminates down a path or sideways into a portico. It is both discreet and resilient.*

Opposite right Pod Lens, *designed by Ross Lovegrove in 1998 for Luceplan, with injection-moulded polycarbonate, integral prismatic lens and over-moulded sides. Primarily intended as an outdoor light, the material is resistant to the elements. The light comes in various colours and fittings with different lengths of stem and base configurations.*

Left Solar Bud, *designed by Ross Lovegrove in 1998 for Luceplan. Solar energy powers the re-chargeable batteries. It is made from natural aluminium and the head is transparent polycarbonate.*

Right *Illuminated bollards are good for path illumination, especially if there are no fixing walls available. Usually very sturdy, they provide good perimeter security too.*

The great thing about outdoor lighting is that it can be temporary and the opportunities for creativity are boundless. Flaming torches, for example, can be used to good effect. Too little is often better than too much, all you are trying to do is guide and flatter. Trying to provide even ambient lighting or high-level bright floodlights outdoors will all too easily look more like security precautions for an open prison.

Luton Sixth Form College
Learning Resources Centre

room effects

The quality of light is directly related to quality of life. By day or by night the effect of light has a profound – if subconscious – effect on the perceptions of space in any environment.

Good lighting can make the prosaic palatial. Any skilled lighting designer can, I guarantee you, turn the most humble of environments into a dramatic *pièce de resistance*. (Domestic practicality may be another issue.) Experience and skill can make a graveyard capable of seeming a fairground and vice versa.

Light can relax, disorientate and stimulate, but as with all good things too much is as bad as too little. The quality of light can be directly related to quality of life.

One has only to think of summer as opposed to winter where the principal difference between the seasons is, in fact, light driven. There is also a profound effect of light on the perceptions of space in any environment.

There are a few simple rules for lighting but many tricks – the only real sin is to expose a naked bulb (nakedness does have a place!), but if you look and try to understand how its magic works you can produce truly amazing results, for surprisingly little effort.

The surroundings will inevitably colour the light reflected off them. Equally, colouring the light will colour the surroundings. An all-white room with white light reflects a large amount of evenly diffused light with the consequence of practically eradicating all shadows and making subtle tonal plays throughout the room. Difficult to keep clean, maybe, but not easy to lose things under a sofa or in a dark corner. The most noticeable impact is the apparent maximization of the illusion of space.

An all-white room also reduces visual clutter and provides a neutral environment where people or art introduce the colour. Small, coloured, low-output lights and vividly coloured objects stand out dramatically, chiming with each other where they might have been lost in a busier space.

Another advantage of the white environment is that it's easy to colourmatch; an interesting and dramatic contrast is to have a strongly primary or black bedroom or a tiny loo (remember not to attempt to use reflected light in these circumstances).

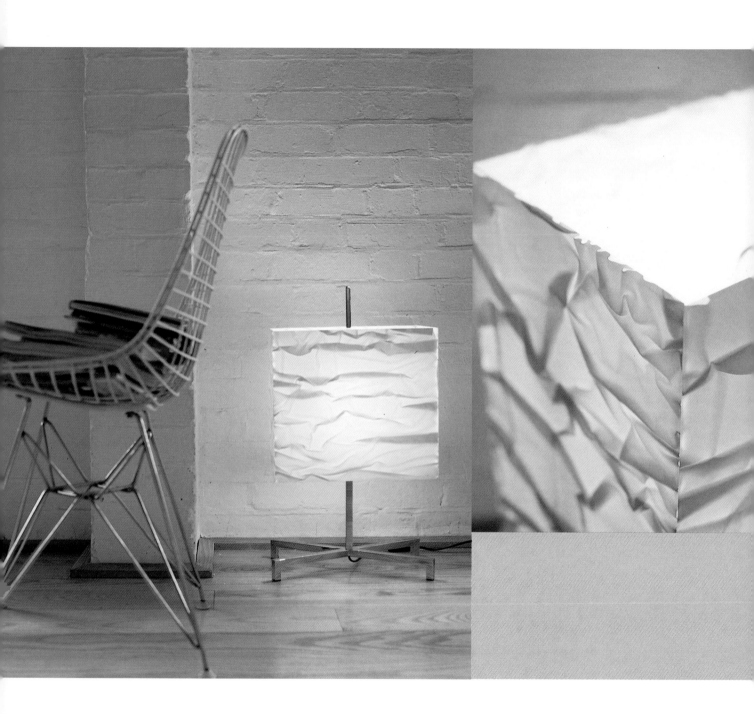

Diffused light shone through a textured surface increases interest and reduces the blandness of the light. Heavily textured walls obliquely lit from the side or low down makes coarse brick work look interesting.

Putting a standard lamp into a corner works well in white or pale rooms as the light bounces off the walls enhancing the illusion of space. In bedrooms it is essential to have some well-positioned light sources that can throw light on to anything you are reading.

Used centrally in a room, a glowing object with a diffuse light source creates useful localized ambient light. It can be especially effective used low down, in corners, next to walls or on tables. It's important to consider what a space will look like in both day and night and plan the lighting accordingly – always consider what effect a piece of lighting equipment will have on its environment when it is turned off during daylight, as well as when turned on. Sculptural forms that reflect light during the day and emit at night are a good example of the need to enhance in either mode – lights can look good filling in supplementing daylight too.

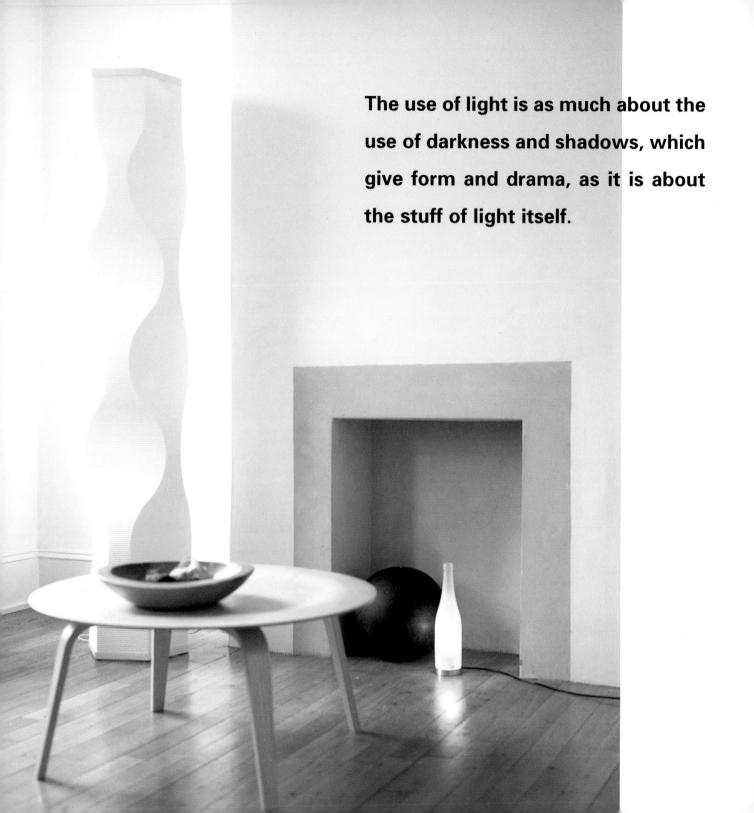

The use of light is as much about the use of darkness and shadows, which give form and drama, as it is about the stuff of light itself.

Colour is a very important issue too; keeping a controlled colour story will give any environment a strong identity. Colour effects can be supplemented by a subtly coloured light, which gives added interest to the coloured objects and walls. Avoid completely bright primary colours unless you are looking to decorate with a toyshop or nursery effect.

Using semi-opaque lamp shades hides the glare of the light source while channelling the light up to the ceiling and down on to the horizontal surfaces producing pleasing, glowing pools of light which add warmth to a room full of otherwise subdued light. This is why this type of lampshade is constantly used so often in reception room environments; the trick is to make it look contemporary – not like the abode of an aged aunt.

Small lights make excellent and thoughtful gifts for many occasions. Scented candles have traditionally made good gifts when visiting someone's home. They are a pleasure to receive – you don't have to rush off to arrange them like a bunch of flowers – and easy to pass on to others if you get caught out (an ancient and revered tradition).

Small lights that owe their existence to their quirky design add charm and give pleasure. Little lights dotted about like tiny dancing fairies can fill out and add interest to low-level ambient light. Candles and nightlights are especially useful for this – the primary purpose of these lights is to add a little zest rather than light with a practical use. When the predominant ambient light is turned low they can spring out becoming much more apparent.

contemporary

designers

achille castiglioni

Achille Castiglioni could be said to be the Godfather of contemporary lighting. He was born in 1918 in Milan, Italy, the youngest of three brothers, all of whom became professional architects and designers. He started off designing in partnership with his elder brother Pier Giacomo and together they had a strong influence on the Flos lighting company from its foundation in 1962. They were one of the first companies to use low-voltage automotive type lamps for domestic lighting with the seminal *Toio* telescopic up-lighting floor lamp (see page 45).

Design can be quite charming in its attempt to communicate ideas and Achille Castiglioni's work is typical of this. Timelessness, innovation, lateral thinking, wit, ingenuity and unpredictability are ingredients in all his work. This said, unlike many designers there is no discernible personal style running through Achille Castiglioni's work – instead, each piece has its own individual strong character.

Brera S, designed for Flos in 1992. This simple and elegant blown glass and plastic construction uses an incandescent bulb to light. This lamp head can be used in a variety of permutations: pendant, wall, ceiling, floor and table.

Left *Diabolo, designed by Flos in 1998 and made of spun aluminium. This pendant light hides 1.5m of flex in the upper cone and can be pulled down to extend by this amount.*

Below middle *Noce, designed in 1972 for Flos. This gigantic, oversized bulkhead light has an enamelled aluminium base and pressed clear glass diffuser.*

Below right *Luminator, designed by Achille and Pier Giacomo Castiglioni in 1954 for Flos. This floor lamp uplighter gives indirect light and was one of the first fittings designed around the integrated reflector mushroom spot lamp. It remains a fresh piece of design.*

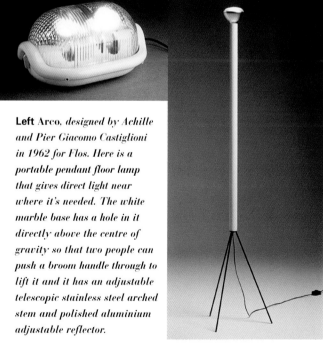

Left *Arco, designed by Achille and Pier Giacomo Castiglioni in 1962 for Flos. Here is a portable pendant floor lamp that gives direct light near where it's needed. The white marble base has a hole in it directly above the centre of gravity so that two people can push a broom handle through to lift it and it has an adjustable telescopic stainless steel arched stem and polished aluminium adjustable reflector.*

ingo maurer

Ingo Maurer was born in 1932 in Germany. For many years he worked as a designer in the USA before returning to Europe in the early 1980s to specialize in lighting design. Ingo Maurer initially explored the opportunities offered by miniature low-voltage dichroic-quartz halogen lamps with his

ground-breaking *Ya Ya Ho* lighting system 1984), which had two parallel wires carrying either terminal of a 12-volt circuit which was both innovative and effective. Since then he has produced more and more seemingly outrageous but often quite seminal design pieces. He has always continued to explore the boundaries of available technology and incorporate it into his work in increasingly imaginative and ingenious ways.

Many lighting designers have what might be best described as a somewhat eccentric personality compared to those concerned with the more tangible and Maurer is best known for his light-hearted and whimsical approach. Often it is closer to an art installation than design – and even then it's not so much sculpture as physical light-emitting poetry. This said, he does have a canny eye for the practical side too, making designs viable but without losing any of his wonderful child-like imagination.

Left *Wo bist du, Edison?, designed in 1997. When is a light not a light? When it's a hologram. A circle of holographic film catches the light emitted by a dichroic reflector housed in a holder modelled on the Edison bulb profile. The effect is to create a mysterious mirage of a glowing light bulb.*

Right *Zettel'z, designed in 1997 with stainless steel, heat resistant satin-frosted glass and Japanese paper. This self-customizable light is created from a kit of parts which invites the user to participate in its final incarnation.*

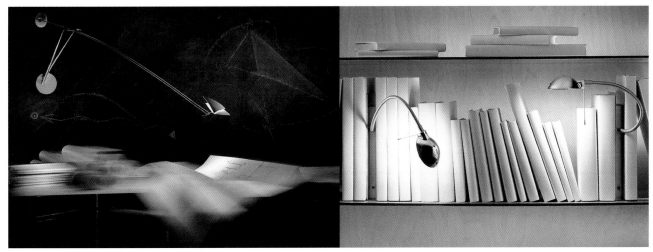

Clockwise, from top left Tijuca Wall, *designed in 1989. Reminiscent of a miniature Sydney Opera House on the end of an articulated fishing rod, these wall-mounted task lights have a good bedside manner. Oskar, designed in 1998. Made of anodized aluminium, these electric book worms neatly nestle among the great authors on your book shelf. Light Structure, designed with Peter Hamburger, the plastic canopy is homage to the design guru* Buckminster Fuller. Savoie, *designed with Donato Savoie in 1979. The canopy and socket are made in white porcelain, housing a semi-frosted bulb. Pierre Ou Paul, designed in 1996, is a massive, height-adjustable aluminium shade, hand-guilded internally. Bellissima Bruta, designed in 1998. This new, extraordinary piece was launched as a one-off at the Milan Design Fair in 1999. It is a showcase of the latest electronic lighting control technology.*

philippe starck

Philippe Starck was born in Paris in 1949 and the best way to describe this ultra-prolific designer is mad-genius-showman. Predictably unpredictable, he works in all fields of design including lighting, interiors, furniture, products and graphics – he has even designed motorcycles and scooters. Originally trained as an architect, he is now probably best known for the charismatic forms of his furniture and domestic artefacts, especially his lights.

Without constraint he seems to have single-handedly created a recognizable, flamboyant, international design style, which combines strong conceptual ideas, functional ingenuity, wit and provocative form with an astonishing attention to detail. Not only does he look for innovative design solutions, he combines them with an exploration of materials and process technology. The boldness of his often-irreverent approach together with the sheer volume of his work has made him perhaps the best-known and most noticed designer alive today.

The originality and lack of compromise evident in his work sometimes meant that it did not gain immediate public acceptance. However, his influence on all areas of the design industry and contemporary design is difficult to refute. Perhaps he could be better described as a sort of court jester with his ability to imaginatively address real design issues in a charmingly light-hearted but gutsy manner.

Below Miss Sissi, *designed by Philippe Starck in 1991 for Flos. This miniature table lamp is made in brightly coloured, beautifully moulded plastic. It is both inexpensive and useful giving direct light up and down and some coloured diffused light to the side.*

Above left Luci Fair, *designed in 1989 for Flos.*

Above centre Le Maire, *designed in 1998 for Kartell. This almost invisible transparent dining chair is made from polycarbonate which is scratch- and shock-resistant – as used in riot shields and bullet proof glass.*

Left Romeo Moon *floor version, designed in 1998 for Flos (see page 43).*

Above Light Lite, *designed in 1992 for Flos. A pendant light giving diffused light with a fluorescent bulb is made from a plastic diffuser and reflector with translucent injection-moulded, coloured plastic inserts. It is available in four different colour combinations.*

Left Ara, *designed in 1988 for Flos. Horn of plenty, horn of light, this chromium-plated table lamp has a lens giving direct light and an integrated tilt switch in the structure that responds to movement in the lamp head.*

tom dixon

Born in Tunisia in 1959, Tom Dixon started adult life as bass guitarist in the soul band Funkapolitan, but after breaking his arm on a motorbike he was unable to swing his arm with quite the same verve. Deciding to become a design star instead, he learned how to weld and in 1985 he inaugurated Creative Salvage; a one-man movement that made furniture from found objects such as car parts, kitchen pans and cast-iron railings. In 1987, he then established the Dixon PID studio-workshop and by 1990 he was recognized as an internationally renowned design force and started designing lights. An excellent example of his individual approach is the pendant light on page 69, which is clearly similar in form to a child's football with a load of styrofoam cups stuck to it!

One charming thing about Tom is that he is far cleverer than he thinks he is, delivering originality again and again and again. Once the self-styled *enfant terrible* of the design scene, he is now the design director of that international design-led, home-store emporium Habitat. His influence and canny vision will no doubt give the company a point of difference that will reposition it as a benchmark of affordable style and practicality. Innovation, daring, lateral thinking and charismatic style are all key ingredients of his work.

Left Star Lights, *designed in 1990. Here is a lightweight steel rod construction covered with Japanese paper to enclose a conventional incandescent bulb.*

Right S Chair, *designed in 1991/92 for Cappellini. Tom Dixon does not limit his talents to lighting design. Here is one of his furniture pieces made from woven marsh reed over a mild steel welded framework.*

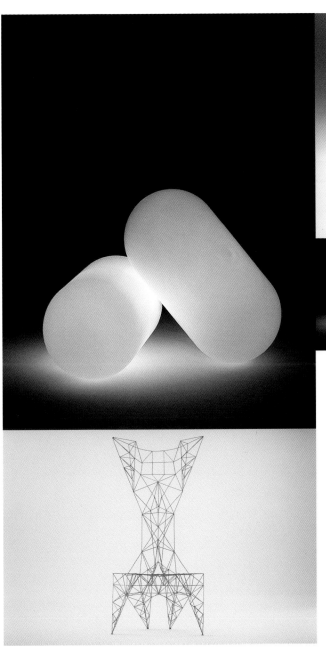

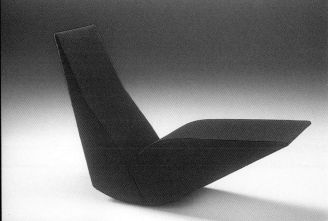

Above Bird, *designed in 1991 for Cappellini. Here is a padded chaise longue covered in wool to disguise its steel frame. It rocks a little disconcertingly when you first alight, but fortunately it quickly becomes reassuringly stable.*

Left Melon, *designed in 1997 for Eurolounge. Looking like giant pills, these luminous, phosphorescent, rotationally-moulded polyethylene capsules work well in multiples.*

Above Star *(see page 69).*

Left Pylon Chair, *designed in 1992 for Cappellini. Inspired by early 'wire frame' computer drawings, this painted mild steel rod construction chair is surprisingly comfortable.*

Right *More* Star Lights *(see opposite).*

Below right Space Projector, *designed by the in-house team at Mathmos. The space projector base and body on this occasional light are made of ABS while the focusing lens and slide carrier are made of nylon.*

factfile tips on buying lights

Planning is the key.

✳ Foresee any installation requirements. For example, some lighting requires transformers that need to be either hidden or contained and many wall lights will need to have wiring traced into the wall and then plastered over.

✳ Decide on whether you want the light source to be a visible feature or camouflaged/hidden from view. Art galleries, for example, are mostly designed so that the light source does not detract from the artwork on the walls.

✳ Take into consideration whether you want, say, task lighting or decorative lighting; or task lighting or ambient lighting, or a combination. Certain tasks require a certain standard level of illuminance for safety reasons.

✳ Consider the reflective, directive and bouncing qualities of light. If you have mirrors behind your lighting, the strength of the bulb may not need to be so high. The colour of the walls behind the lights will also affect the quality, as lighter colours will reflect and darker colours will absorb the light.

✳ Check the compatibility and availability of bulbs.

✳ Check the plug and socket compatibility: different countries have different requirements.

✳ Plan to use dimmers whenever possible as they add flexibility to your lighting scheme. Dimmers for adjustable levels of ambient light in the bathroom are also useful. But ensure the switches are outside the room.

✳ Dimmers reduce light but do not save electricity much so use a lower wattage bulb.

✳ Install at least some of the light control systems by the main door so you don't have to stumble in or out of a dark room.

✳ Balance task lighting with ambient light to avoid shadows on hands.

✳ Safety and stability are important. Free-standing uplighters can be hazards when children and pets are around.

✳ Lights can also be fire hazards – items falling on or into bulbs can catch alight, causing glass and bulb to explode.

✳ Take environmental concerns into account: save electricity by attaching timers or sensors on to some key lights for when you are out of the home.

✳ The key difference between the various bulb options is their efficiency and the quality and quantity of light they emit. Here is a comparison of lamp efficiencies:

Description	Average life	Temperature	Light output	Energy efficiency
100W incandescent globe	1,000 hours	2,500°C	1,200 lumens	12 lumens/watt
100W tungsten filament	2,000 hours	2,500°C	1,200 lumens	12 lumens/watt
500W quartz-halogen	3,000 hours	2,800°C	9,500 lumens	19 lumens/watt
65W fluorescent tube	9,000 hours	2,900°C	5,000 lumens	76 lumens/watt
18W compact fluorescent tube	10,000 hours	2,900°C	1,500 lumens	83 lumens/watt

The compact fluorescent tube is almost seven times more energy efficient than the tungsten filament lamp, albeit at the expense of light quality.

stockists & designers

The following stores stock a good range of contemporary lighting. If you are looking for a particular piece, it is worth telephoning the store first to check they still carry the range.

ARKITYPE DESIGN PARTNERSHIP
BerkleyStreet
Glasgow G3 7HH
Tel: 0141 248 8623

AKTIVA
10b Spring Place
Kentish Town
London NW5 3BH
Tel: 020 7428 9325

ALTIMA LIGHTING LTD
2-10 Telford Way
London W3 7Xs
Tel: 020 8600 3500

ARIA
295 Upper Street
London N1 2TU
Tel: 020 7704 1999
Range includes lighting by: Philippe Starck, Spirello, Lava lamps

ARTWORKS
2-22 Upper Street
London N1 0PQ
Tel: 020 7354 1114
Range includes lighting by: Flos

ATRIUM LTD
Centrepoint
22-24 St Giles High Street
London WC2H 8LN
Tel: 020 7379 7288

BABYLON DESIGN LTD
301 Fulham Road
London SW10 9QH
Tel: 020 7376 7255

BOND PROJECTS UK LTD
Prism Design Studio
38 Grosvenor Gardens
London SW1W 0EB
Tel: 020 7730 3011

BOWLES AND LINARES
32 Hereford Road
London W2 5AJ
Tel: 020 7229 9886

PETER BURIAN ASSOCS
International Lighting
Hillview
Vale of Heath
London NW3 1AN
Tel: 020 7431 2345
Lighting consultants

CATALYTICO
Basement Level
1-3 St Leonard s Road
London EC2A 4AQ
Tel: 020 7225 1720
Range includes lighting by: Ingo Maurer, Foscarini, Luceplan

CENTRAL
33-35 Little Clarendon Street
Oxford OX1 2HU
Tel: 01865 311141
Range includes lighting by: Catelitico, Bulge Trading Co, Driade, Kartell

CHAPPEAU CLAUDETTE
15 Hereward Road
London SW17 7EY
Tel: 020 8877 9192

Maglite torch.

CLEMENTE CAVIGIOLI
5 Walmer Studios
235-239 Walmer Road
London W11 4EY
Tel: 020 7792 2522
UK agent for Fontana Arte Group

CLEMENTINE HOPE
73 Bread Street
Edinburgh EH3 9AH
Tel: 0131 221 1700

CO-EXISTENCE
288 Upper Street
London N1 2TZ
Tel: 020 7354 8817
Range includes lighting by:
Artemide, Flos, Fontana Arte,
Luceplan, Valvono Design,
Pallucco Italia

CONRAN COLLECTION
12 Conduit Street
London W1S 2XQ
Tel: 020 7399 0710

CONRAN SHOP
Michelin House
81 Fulham Road
London SW3 6RD
Tel: 020 7589 7401
and
55 Marylebone High Street
London W1M 3AE
Tel: 020 7723 2223
Range includes lighting by:
Artemide, Fontana Arte,
Foscarini, Luceplan, Paolo
Rizzatto, Achille/Pier Giacomo
Castiglioni, Babylon Design,
Richard Sapper, Flos, Peter
Wylly, Phillippe Stark

CONRAN & PARTNERS
22 Shad Thames
London SE1 2YU
Tel: 020 7403 0099
Design consultants

COTTERELS LIGHTING
28-35 Carnhouse Place
Glasgow
Tel: 0141 225 2888

DESIGN SHOP
10 Richmond Hill
Richmond
Surrey TW10 6QX
Tel: 020 8241 2421
Range includes lighting by: Poul
Henningsen, Vico Magistretti,
Jasper Morrison, Richard Sapper,
Ross Lovegrove, Aero, Artemide,
Flos, Kartell, O Luce, Philippe
Starck, Achille/Pier Giacomo
Castiglioni

EL ULTIMO GRITO
26 Northfield House
Frensham Street
London SE15 6TL
Tel: 020 7732 6614

EUROLOUNGE
28 All Saints Road
London W11 1HG
Tel: 020 7792 5499
Range includes lighting by: Tom
Dixon

HABITAT
Tel: 0845 60 10 740
For nearest store
Range includes lighting by:
Babylon Design, Flos,
Peter Wylly

IKEA
Tel: 020 8208 5600
For nearest store

INFLATE
28 Exmouth Market
London EC1R 4QE
Tel: 020 7251 5453

INHOUSE
24-26 Wilson Street
Glasgow G1 1SS
Tel: 0141 552 5902

and
28 Howe Street
Edinburgh EH3 6TG
Tel: 0131 225 2888
Range includes lighting by: Flos,
Ingo Maurer, O Luce, Fontana Arte

JEREMY LORD, THE
COLOUR LIGHT COMPANY
12 Craycombe Farm
Fladbury
Pershore
Worcs WR10 2QS
Tel: 01386 861086

MATHMOS
Mail order through Mathmos
direct on Tel: 020 7549 2743
Or through showrooms listed
below:
179 Drury Lane
London WC2B

20-24 Old Street
London EC1V 9AP

Sterte Avenue West
Poole
Dorset BH15 2BD

MDS
Unit 9 , Hewitts Industrial Estate
Elmbridge Road
Cranleigh
Surrey GU6 8LW
Tel: 01483 276206

MICHAEL MARRIOTT
Units No 4 & 6
Ellsworth Street
Bethnal Green
London E2 0AX

MODULAR UK
Tel: 020 7681 9953
Range includes lighting by:
Fontana, Arte, Foscarini, Daniela
Puppa, Richard Sapper

MUNKENBECK &
MARSHALL
3 Pine Street
London EC1
Tel: 020 7833 1407
Architects in light

NEW ROOMS
51 High Street
Cheltenham
Gloucester
GL50 1DX
Tel: 01242 2379777
Range includes lighting by: Aero,
Flos, Inflate, Kartell, Philippe
Starck, Achille Castiglioni

NICEHOUSE
The Italian Centre Courtyard
Ingram Street
Glasgow G1 1DN
Tel: 0141 553 1377

PURVES & PURVES
220–224 Tottenham Court Road
London W1P 9HD
Tel: 020 7580 8223
Range includes lighting by:
Babylon Design, Flos, Fontana
Arte, Proto Design, Charles
Williams, Jasper Morrison,
Philippe Starck

RALPH CAPPER
INTERIORS
10a Little Peter Street
Manchester M16 4PS
Tel: 0161 236 6929
Range includes lighting by:
Artemide, Flos

ROUND THE WORLD
15 Northwest Circus Place
Edinburgh
Tel: 0131 225 7800

SAME
146 Brick Lane
London E1 6RV
Tel: 020 7247 9992

SCP
135-139 Curtain Road
London EC2A 3BX
Tel: 020 7739 1869

SET
100 High Street
Leicester LE1 5YP
Tel: 0116 251 0161
*Range includes lighting by: Flos,
Alva, DPG, Inflate, Babylon
Design, Michael Sodeau,
Artemide (will source others)*

SKK
34 Lexington Street
London W1R 3HR
Tel: 020 7434 4095
*Range includes lighting by: Shiu-
Kay Kan, Flos, Mathmos*

SPACE
214 Westbourne Gove
London W11 2RH
Tel: 020 7229 6533
*Range includes lighting by:
Caterina Fadda, Castiglioni*

TANGRAM
3 Dundas Street
Edinburgh
Tel: 0131 225 6551

**THE LONDON LIGHTING
COMPANY**
135 Fulham Road
London SW3 6RT
Tel: 020 7589 3612
*Range includes lighting by:
Kartell, Louis Poulsen, Mathmos,
Michele de Lucchi, Paolo
Rizzatto, Poul Henningsen*

VIADUCT FURNITURE LTD
1-10 Summers Street
London EC1R 5BD
Tel: 020 7278 8456
*Range includes lighting by:
Artemide, Bowles & Linares,
Classicon, Snowcrash, Caterina
Fadda, Peter Wylly*

28 LIGHTING
28 East Street
Saffron Walden
Essex CB10 1LS
Tel: 01799 522133

Auction houses

BONHAMS
Montpelier Street
London SW7 1HH
Tel: 020 7393 3900
and
65-69 Lots Road
London SW10 0RN
Tel: 020 7351 7111

CHRISTIE'S
8 Kings Street
London SW1Y 6QT
Tel: 020 7839 9060
and
85 Old Brompton Road
London SW7 3LD
Tel: 020 7581 7611

SOTHEBY'S
34-35 New Bond Street
London W1A 2AA
Tel: 020 7293 5000

Places to visit

CRAFTS COUNCIL
44a Pentonville Road
London N1 9BY
Tel: 020 7278 770

DESIGN MUSEUM
Butlers Wharf
28 Shad Thames
London SE1 2YD
Tel: 020 7403 6933

GEFFRYE MUSEUM
Kinsland Road
London E2 8EA
Tel: 020 7739 9893

GLASGOW SCHOOL OF ART
167 Renfrew Street
Glasgow
Tel: 0141 353 4500

**HILLHEAD
HOUSE/HUNTERIAN ART
GALLERY**
University of Glasgow
Hillhead Street
Glasgow
Tel: 0141 330 5431

THE SCIENCE MUSEUM
Exhibition Road
London SW7 2DD
Tel: 020 7938 8000

**THE TWENTIETH
CENTURY GALLERY**
Victoria & Albert Museum
Cromwell Road
London SW7 2RL
Tel: 020 7938 8500

Further reading

*The following books provide
more detailed information on
contemporary design and
lighting and the individual
designers mentioned in this book.*

Mel Byars: *50 Lights, Innovations
in Design and Materials*
Pro Design Series, Rotovision
ISBN 88046 265 7

Tom Dixon
Architecture, Design and
Technology Press, 1990
ISBN 18 5454 8425

Phillippe Garner: *Sixties Design*
Benedikt Taschen Verlag GmbH
ISBN 3 8228 8934 2
Lynn Gordon: *ABC of Design*
Chronicle Books, 1996
ISBN 0 8118 1141 7

Jean Gorman: *Detailing Light*
Whitney, 1995
ISBN 0 8230 1341 3

Thomas Hauffe: *Design: A
Concise History*
Lawrence King, 1998
ISBN 1 856 69134 9

Wanda Jankowski: *Creative
Lighting*
PBC International PLC, 1997
ISBN 0 86636 343 2

Peta Levi: *New British Design
1998*
Mitchel Beazley, 1988
ISBN 1 84000 099 6

Licht/Light Design
Stichting/Foundation, 1998
ISBN 90 76497 01 X

Jeremy Myerson: *International
Lighting Design*
Lawrence King, 1996
ISBN 85669 0865

Pocket Design Directory
Janvier Publishing, 1998
ISBN 0 95184 949 2

Renny Ramakers and Giss Bakker
(eds): *Droog Design, Spirit of the
Nineties*, OIO Publishers
ISBN 90 6450 301 X

Starck
Benedikt Taschen Verlag GmbH
ISBN 3 8228 8500 2

Peter Tregenza and David Loe:
The Design of Lighting
E & FN Spon, 1998
ISBN 0 419 204407

Janet Turner: *Designing with
Light*, Rotovision, 1998
ISBN 2 88046 334 3

WITHDRAWN

index

WITHDRAWN
Luton Sixth Form College
Learning Resources Centre

First published in Great Britain in 1999 by
Conran Octopus Ltd
a part of Octopus Publishing Group
2–4 Heron Quays, London E14 4JP
www.conran-octopus.co.uk

This paperback edition published in 2003

ISBN 1 84091 316 9

Text copyright © Sebastian Conran and Mark Bond 1999
Design and layout copyright © Conran Octopus Ltd 1999
Special photography copyright © Thomas Stewart 1999

All rights reserved. No part of this book may be reproduced,
stored in a retrieval system or transmitted, in any form or by
any means, electronic, electrostatic, magnetic tape,
mechanical, photocopying, recording or otherwise, without
the prior permission in writing of the Publisher.

The right of Sebastian Conran and Mark Bond to be identified
as Authors of the text of this Work has been asserted by them
in accordance with the Copyright,
Designs and Patents Act 1988

Commissioning Editor Denny Hemming
Series Editor Gillian Haslam
Project Editor Emma Callery
Managing Editor Kate Bell
Index Emma Callery

Creative Director Leslie Harrington
Art Editor Lucy Gowans
Stylists Emma Thomas and Sarah Hollywood
Production Zoe Fawcett

British Library Cataloguing-in-Publication Data.
A catalogue record for this book is available from
the British Library.

Colour origination by Sang Choy International, Singapore

Printed in China

Acknowledgments

Special thanks for Tim Gadd for research and for all his help behind the
scenes. Thanks also to Peter Burian, Kathryn Mills and Alfred Munkenbeck.

The authors and publishers wish to thank the following for their
considerable help and assistance: Josie Ballin at **Mathmos**; Gilla Bond
at **Artemide**; Sharon Bowles at **Bowles and Linares**; Tamara Caspersz
and James Mair at **Viaduct**; Clemente Cavigioli; Sophie Chandler;
Norman Cull at **Number 16**; Fiona Dodd at **Same**; Joao Ferreira at **Proto
UK**; Elena Graves at **Eurolounge**; Clementine Hope; Andrew Johnson
and Gill Hicks at **Blueprint**; Frank Kelly at **MDS**; Joanne Leyland at
Purves & Purves; Jeremy Lord; Fiona Mackenzie-Jenkin at **Inflate**;
Michael Marriott; Alexis Nishihata at **Aero**; Dennis Ong at **Aktiva**;
James Peto at **Design Museum**; Suzel Pitty at **Babylon**; Roy Sant;
Vanessa Scheibner at **Tecta**; Jo Wolley at **Catalytico**.

With thanks for the following for the kind loan of transparencies:
Aero (p.70 Paper Pendant, p.71 Anywhere Light), **Anglepoise**
/www.anglepoise.co.uk (p.17), **Aram Design** (p.17 Grey), **Aktiva** (p.54
Filo, Swivel, p.71 Filo Pendant, p.78 Search Light SL-111, p.87 Icon
'Holes' & Search Light), **Artemide** (p.17 Magistretti & Sapper, p.46 Iride
& Latona, p.60 Shogun, p.79 Musa Sospensione, p.80 Mikado Track &
Chronocolour Series, p.88 Acheo, p.93 Pantarei 300 Half Light), **Babylon**
(p.75 UFL), **Box** (p.76 Waves), **Sophie Chandler** (p.57 Lightbowl 1, 2),
Sebastian Conran (p.90 & 92), **David Design** (p.46 Lowlight and
Highlight), **Tom Dixon** (p.118 portrait of Tom Dixon & Star Lights, p.119
Pylon Chair, Star Lights & Bird), **Flos** (p.17 Castiglioni, p.23 Fucsia, p.30
Wall Light, p.41, p.42 Taccia, p.46 Helice, p.55 Miss Sissi, p.71 Cina,
p.72-73 Fucsia, p.78 Romeo Moon 52, p.83 Lastra 6, p.85 Ariette, p.86
Wall A Wall A & Train Train, p.87 Drop 2, p.110 Brera S, all of p.112-113,
p.116 Miss Sissi, p.117 Lucifair, Light Lite & Ara), **Fontana Arte** (p.17
Chiesa, p.43 Elvis, p.50 '2198', p.55 '2198 TA', p.66 Ray, p.75 Alzaia),
Foscarini (p.50 bottom left, p.88 Circus Grande), **Clementine Hope** (p.74
Light Light), **Inflate** (p.75 UFO), **Jeremy Lord** (p.86 Chromawall),
Pearson Lloyd (p.55 Ilos), **Luceplan** (p.42 Costanza & Pod Lens, p.46
Lola floor & Lucilla, p.55 On Off, p.66 Fortebraccio, p.78 Titania, p.87
Lola Wall, p.88 Screen, p.93 Solar Bud, p.93 Pod Lens), **Mathmos** (p.60
Fibre Space, p.62 Lava Lamp, p.121 Space Projector) **Ingo Maurer** (p.14
Fly Candle Fly, p.75 Zuuk, p.80 Ya Ya Ho, p.89 Zero One, p.111 Oskar, all
of p.114-115), **Jasper Morrison** (p.80 Glo Ball Pendant) **Pallucco Italia**
(p.17 Fortuny, p.47 Short Wave Long Wave), **Lucy Pope** (p.89 Rubber
Light), **Proto UK** (p.70 Pendant Light), **Louis Poulsen** (p.17 Henningsen,
p.29, p.67, p.81 PH Snowball & Satellite Pendant), **Purves & Purves**
(p.117 La Maire, Romeo Moon floor version), Roy Sant (p.71 Daisy),
Tecta (p.17 Rietvelt), **Nic Tompkin** (p.8 & 11).

Thanks for the following for the loan of accessories for photography:
Alma Leather (020 7375 0343), **Century Design** (020 7487 5100),
Co-existence (020 7354 8817), **Grasslands & Savanah** (020 7727 4727),
Mathmos (020 7549 2700), **Purves & Purves** (020 7580 8223), **Robert
Wyatt** (020 8530 6891), **Same** (0171 247 9992), **Sixty 6** (020 7224 6066),
Shiu-Kay Kan (020 7434 4095), **Space** (020 7229 6533), **Stepan
Tertsakian** (020 7236 8788), **Viaduct** (020 7278 8456), **Walkahead**
(020 7275 8908).